eCommerce Marketing

HOW TO DRIVE TRAFFIC THAT BUYS TO YOUR WEBSITE

Chloë **Thomas**

Copyright information

© Copyright Chloë Thomas, 2013

Published 2013
Kernu Publishing
Windsor House
12–14 High Street
Kidlington
OX5 2DH
United Kingdom

ISBN 978-0-9573128-6-9

Cover photograph: © Jacqueline Cross Photographer
www.JacquelineCrossPhotography.com

Cover and interior design: Visual Philosophy Ltd
www.VisualPhilosophy.com

Illustrations: Joni McPherson, McPherson Graphics,
www.McPhersonGraphics.com

Printed in the United Kingdom by TJ International, Cornwall, UK

Praise for *eCommerce Marketing*

'*eCommerce Marketing* by Chloë Thomas is a must-read for anyone looking to improve and build an eCommerce business. This book is an easy step-by-step guide to building and structuring your online business. Chloë has made it so easy to pick up and dip in and out of sections of the book that are relevant to your own business needs.

After reading Chloë's *eCommerce MasterPlan* book, I was thrilled to hear she was writing a follow-up. Being fairly new to the eCommerce world, these books have been a great help in learning and developing my knowledge and keeping up to date with the ever-changing eCommerce industry.

I highly recommend this book; not only is it a great read but it also offers plenty of inspiration on how to improve your business with a clear strategy.'

Sophie Hedges, Marketing Manager, Garden Trading
www.gardentrading.co.uk

'Another eCommerce blockbuster from Chloë Thomas. Most books like this tell you what to do, but Chloë's book tells you HOW to do it. This is eCommerce made simple, and tackles vital areas such as social media marketing and how to integrate online and offline marketing.

For seasoned experts, Chloë also brings us her perspective on Remarketing and Partnership marketing, which gives relationships with customers the right priority.

Full of helpful hints and tips and based on experience and statistics, this book needs to be read by anyone who wants to get ahead of the pack in eCommerce.'

Tim Brawn, The Brawn Consultancy

'After reading Chloë's latest book, *eCommerce Marketing*, it is evidently written by someone who not only knows her stuff but has lived it. She has managed to bring together everything into one place as a guide and ongoing reference. For anyone engaged in eCommerce, this book is a must; it will inspire you to test new techniques and hone the ones you're already using.

Any business person, retail or otherwise, that is looking to grow their business will find this book invaluable. Chloë is building a great reputation in the eCommerce sector and books like this are the reason why.'

Wayne Parrott, Royal Mail
www.royalmail.com

'eCommerce Marketing is an essential companion to Chloë Thomas' much acclaimed book the eCommerce Masterplan. Again a complex subject matter has been covered in a concise yet comprehensive manner.

The book covers a fast moving and evolving topic, but Chloe has brought together the core essentials to give readers a firm grounding from which to develop and refine their techniques. It is a welcome addition to the available literature and will save many hours of reading through conflicting and confusing advice online.'

Peter Blackler, Insignia Creative
www.insigniacreative.co.uk

'Chloë's new book provides you with a step-by-step road map to how to get more traffic to your website. It is one of the most practical guides to web marketing I have ever read, and manages to de-mystify a subject that can easily become over-complex and mystifying. It is a great tool for those who are not confident about how to develop their on-line strategy, but also gives direction to those who have established strategies but want to refine and develop what they do.

Chloë's background and experience means she really understands the reality of implementing an e-commerce plan, and as well as advising the key areas to focus on, she is not afraid to advise what not to do, which is vital if you have limited time and resources. I find her books and her advice invaluable.'

Jim McDowell, Sarah Raven
www.sarahraven.com

Acknowledgements

· ·

Thank you to everyone who's supported the eCommerce MasterPlan journey so far! Plus, a special mention to Hilary Fletcher of ecco-shoes.co.uk for all her feedback, leading to the creation of Chapter 10.

Thank you.

Chloë Thomas

Contents

· ·

Content is at the heart of any future-proofed online marketing
strategy.

The key tool every eCommerce business needs to master. It
will keep your customers buying from you, it will drive your
sales and it will build your relationship with those customers.

Increasingly important for every business because it impacts
in so many ways. Social media can build brand awareness,
activate offline marketing, distribute your content, power your
search traffic and much more.

Introduction

. . . .

What is eCommerce?

When I talk about eCommerce I mean:

- a business
- selling products or services
- taking the order online

So it could be a business selling thousands of books per month, or it could be a travel agency, or even a kid's party entertainer who takes bookings online.

eCommerce also needn't be the whole business. There are many eCommerce businesses with a wholesale division on the side. There are many "offline" businesses with an eCommerce area – just look at *eCommerce MasterPlan*; some of our products and services you can buy online, others you have to buy face to face or over the phone.

Why an eCommerce MasterPlan?

What Sort of eCommerce Business Are You?
- Identify your eCommerce Business Structure
- Identify the Scale of Your Product Range
- Differentiate your Business

Establishing The Core Foundations
- Build the Right Website
- Build your Business for Profit and Growth
- Select your Products and Promotions

I Have Built It: Why haven't they come? (aka Marketing!)
- Research your Marketing Plan
- Creating your Marketing Plan
- Test, Measure and Optimise your Marketing

eCommerce is a huge, growing industry. In the UK last year it grew by 16%, while Europe remains the biggest eCommerce marketplace. North America is catching up, and the eCommerce market in the Middle East and Australasia are growing fast.

Despite its size and maturity, there is no roadmap for success. There is no easy-to-follow guide that will help eCommerce businesses succeed. I find it highly frustrating seeing great businesses wasting opportunities in eCommerce, and wasting time on the wrong marketing and the wrong website just because they haven't the luxury of the time to research the other options. It's that wasted time, effort, and money that I hope *eCommerce MasterPlan* will help many businesses to avoid.

What is the *eCommerce MasterPlan* Based On?

Since 2001, I have been working in direct marketing, and since 2004 I have been directly involved with the structures and marketing of eCommerce businesses. At the last count, I have been directly involved with the marketing of over 50 eCommerce businesses, some as a member of staff and some as a consultant. I have project-managed more than 15 eCommerce website builds or rebuilds, and advised on many more. I have helped eCommerce businesses launch and go international, and helped high-street retailers launch online.

Unfortunately I have also seen them close or go under, simply because they didn't understand what sort of business they were, or they used the wrong marketing, or invested in the wrong website. All issues it's possible to avoid.

The businesses I've worked for have sold everything from high-street fashion, to books, to holidays, to workshops and downloads. In all that time, I have barely seen two businesses approach eCommerce in the same way; all have done good things, all have done some things badly – teams, structure, products, websites. Almost every business I've looked at is avoiding a marketing method that holds a key to their success, or stubbornly holding on to one that is doing them no favours at all.

What I have learnt along the way is that there are some clear structures that, when followed, invariably lead to success, and some great big potholes that, if you know about them in advance, are really easy to avoid.

The *eCommerce MasterPlan* books are based on all I have learnt from spending my working life immersed in eCommerce. I believe it provides the blueprint, the roadmap, the MasterPlan for the success of every eCommerce business. If you follow the 3 Steps outlined in *eCommerce MasterPlan 1.8: Your 3 Steps to Successful Online Selling* and then plan and optimise your marketing by following the advice contained here in *eCommerce Marketing: How to Drive Traffic that Buys to your Website*, you'll build a very successful eCommerce operation.

You can buy any of the books in the eCommerce MasterPlan series from Amazon, iTunes, any good bookshop – or direct from us at **eCommerceMasterPlan.com/Books**

How to Use this Book

· ·

This book is designed so you can dip in and out of it.

- Focusing on PPC this month? – try Chapter 7
- Social media needing a boost? – head to Chapter 3
- Drowning in data? – time for Chapter 10 and the metrics!

If you are new to eCommerce, I highly recommend you read the whole book before diving into the individual marketing methods you're going to be putting into practice.

eCommerce and online marketing are constantly changing, so the book is designed to help you take the right approach no matter what changes. Of course, though, you need to keep up to date with what's happening and how to use each of the tools: that's where **eCommerceMasterPlan.com** comes in, and throughout the book you'll find the following symbols when there's useful content available for you online:

WORKBOOK

I have created a series of workbooks to help you make the most of each chapter – so make sure you download them to work through alongside the book. If you want to get the workbook for the whole book right now, then just go to **eCommerceMasterPlan.com/Free**

DOWNLOAD
I have also put a lot of useful templates on the website ready for you to download and use. Please do make the most of them when you see this logo!

WEBSITE
When there's some great extra content that will help you on the website, we've used this logo.

GRADUATES
If you've already worked through the first book in the series – *eCommerce MasterPlan* – these sections will help you tie it all together.

Before you go any further, register at **eCommerceMasterPlan.com/ Free** so you've got quick access to all the support materials.

Enjoy!

CHAPTER 1

Content Marketing

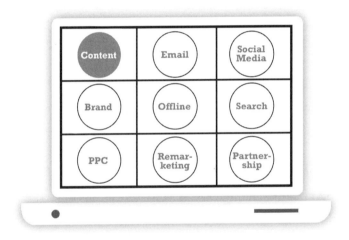

Content marketing is a great way to get traffic from the search engines and other sites. It takes time to see sizable impact, but once working, attracts traffic and builds a loyal customer base.

At its simplest it's a blog and great product pages – but it can then stray into any number of other areas.

GRADUATES

This method is particularly useful for these **eCommerce Business Structures**:

- Online Only
- Boutique Bricks and Clicks
- Niche PiggyBack

It's especially powerful at the Niche end of the **Product Range Scale**. It is also particularly useful if your **USP** (Unique Selling Proposition) is:

- Knowledge and Information – because it's central to building a reputation for knowledge and information.
- Customer Service – part of customer service is providing customers with the information they need.

Why Should You Use Content Marketing if You Are an eCommerce Business?

Major problems for eCommerce websites are a lack of non-selling pages and an inability to convey the values and positioning of the business via a website.

Content marketing not only solves both of these, it also will have a positive impact on many areas of the business:

- Once you have built your content, it's very hard for a competitor to copy you.

- Providing great content will mark your website out as a fantastic source of useful information, not just another eCommerce website, really enhancing your brand and customers' perception of you.
- It provides you with a USP that is very hard to copy.
- Great content is an essential foundation of a social media strategy – social media is all about sharing and conversations. So you need something to talk about and something to share – that's the job of the content.
- It's a way to use the great knowledge that already exists in your business.
- Content is essential to a successful search strategy. It will act as "link bait", encouraging other people to link to your website. It will also provide pages that will attract the search engines and contain lots of keywords.
- Having content will enable your other marketing strategies to be more interesting and drive better results; you'll have something other than products to talk about.
- Finally it will bring you a steady stream of traffic that's interested in your products and business, month in, month out.

However, it does take a lot of time and effort to build a good content base and the task never ends. You must keep building it, too.

. . . .

Content Marketing Objectives for eCommerce Businesses

The impact of your content marketing will be hard to measure – but that's no excuse for not having objectives.

Successful content marketing relies on lots of content and a stream of new content. It may take a long time (6–12 months) before you see real sales gains.

Content will impact on lots of other areas of your marketing, making it hard to isolate and track exactly what impact the content has. Some of its impact will be felt through search, social media and other marketing channels.

The content is there to attract traffic to your website and to create sales activity from that traffic so, as you build content the big numbers should increase – conversion rate, sales, AOV (Average Order Value). That all comes from your content being consumed, that means it's successful, so key objectives need to include how much the content is consumed (the page views, or video watches etc.).

. . . .

How Content Marketing Works

- You put content online
- People consume it
- They like it and tell people about it
- They like it and it makes them trust you more
- More people and more trust = more sales

At its simplest, content marketing is creating content that relates to your brand/products and putting it on your website. That might be a guide to buying the perfect jeans or how to install a dishwasher, it might be an opinion on an article on the solar technology of the future, or just really great product page copy.

Every piece of content you create should do at least one of these things (and usually all of them!):

- Be something people will read and want to share – either by sharing on social media or linking to it
- Reflect your brand well, enhancing it by supporting what you stand for and positioning you as an expert in your field
- Help sell the products – removing barriers to conversion, like a sizing guide, or a catwalk video
- Appeal to your target customers

Content that fits with your business will also help bring you search engine traffic. It creates relevant pages for search engines to get their teeth into and it creates interesting things that people will share on social media. All of that increases your chances of getting traffic from the search engines.

What is content?

Content is anything you put publically online that can be consumed (read, watched, listened to) and shared, so it might be on your site, a blog, your blog – anywhere online. Here are some ideas of what content can be:

- Infographics – these are pictorial displays of data and are very popular. There are lots getting shared already on social media platforms.
- Guest Blogging – this can be a great way to get content, or spread your content. You may want to find someone to guest blog on your website, or go guest blogging yourself. This is a way to increase customers' perception of your expertise.

- Videos – YouTube – the second largest search engine in the world. And it's owned by Google. So if you are creating videos, why not upload them here? You can easily then embed them in your own site too, which saves on hosting costs.
- Photos – there are lots of great photo hosting sites, like Flickr. With Instagram and Pinterest around now, it's also important to make sure your images are easily shared.
- PDFs and Documents – SlideShare and Scribd – these are two sites where you can upload documents to be shared. So how-to guides and presentations are well worth putting up here.
- Your Blog – writing regular updates and opinion pieces.
- FAQs – lists of the most often asked questions, with the answers.
- Buying Guides – useful guides to help your customers.
- Customer Reviews – yes, you don't have to create all the content yourself.

WORKBOOK
There is a workbook for creating your content marketing plan available on the website at
eCommerceMasterPlan.com/Free

What content can you/should you create?

Most businesses have more content than they realise, so before you do anything else you need to work out what content you already have. To do this, you need to brainstorm with key people in the business and start to create a list of what could/should be created. Speak to the owner, buyers, marketing, customer services, merchandising, website team etc. Ask them:

- What content do we already have?
- What content would our customers appreciate having on the website?
- What stories are there around our products?

Take the answers and **extrapolate** them. The chances are that from the brainstorm there won't be a vast number of stories; that's because people are simplifying it. Each story that's on the brainstorm can create several items of content. The mistake everyone makes is to assume one idea is one piece of content.

$$\Big[\textbf{One Idea} \neq \textbf{One Piece of Content} \Big]$$

For example:

Initial Idea = Photo Shoot for Summer Season

Stories =

- Footage of the shoot
- Competition about the shoot – location, models, style it, win the clothes used
- Guess the location
- General excitement piece
- What the models think of the range

Content =

- Video of the shoot
- Backstage photos from the shoot
- Out-takes from the shoot

- Competitions on/for:
    - Facebook
    - Twitter
    - Pinterest
    - email
    - in a partner magazine
    - for bloggers
    - for stylists
- Interview with team prepping it
- Interview with models afterwards – on audio, video, and written

Each idea has the potential to be turned into several different pieces of content in varying formats.

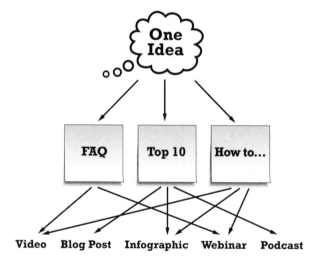

Take all these ideas and plan your content marketing calendar for the year. I've found it works best when there's a rhythm to it. Either focus on one topic per month, or the same thing the first week/second week etc. This might be:

- Month 1 – Product Range A
  - Week 1 FAQs
  - W2 How we selected X
  - W3 Customer testimonials
  - W4 Coming up later this year
- M2 – Product Range B

Or:

- Every month:
  - W1 Content about a key product
  - W2 Content about future new ranges that aren't yet available
  - W3 Improve customer experience – FAQs, better product page copy etc.
  - W4 Content from a keen customer/expert/opinion piece

Decide your content formats and what platforms you are going to use

Now you have an idea of the sort of content you are going to be creating, you need to decide what formats, and what platforms, you are going to be using.

For most businesses, the starting point, the centre of your content strategy, is your blog. A blog can host pictures, text, audio, and video which makes it really versatile. Plus you own it entirely – beir means it's all working for you.

Top Tip
Where to Put the Blog

Ideally it should be located at www.yourdomain.com/blog; then the search engines see it as part of your website. If you can't do that for hosting reasons, then use blog.yourdomain.com: this will be classed as a separate website by the search engines, so you need to make sure you have plenty of links back to the eCommerce website.

Blog content is very easy to syndicate and feed into your social media activity using RSS feeds.

If you are creating video, audio, images, presentations, etc., then to get the most from them you should be putting the content on popular websites as well as your own:

- Video => YouTube
- Photos => Flickr
- Audio => YourListen.com
- Presentations => SlideShare or Scribd

This will get your content in front of many more people and start driving people to your website, not just attracting them in – getting you much more exposure.

WEBSITE
Find a guide on where to put different types of content on websites PLUS information on how to use RSS Feeds at **eCommerceMasterPlan.com/Free**

Now you have a list of where you are going to be putting your content. We need to merge that into the content marketing calendar.

Add a row for each content method you'll be using this year and then mark which item is going where. So one week you might have content going everywhere, the next just a blog.

	A	B	C	D	E	F	G	H
1	Content Calendar 20xx							
2								
3								
4			January				February	
5		1	2	3	4	1	2	3
6	Idea							
7	Stories							
8	Blogs							
9	Videos							
10	Other							

DOWNLOAD

There's an example promo calendar you can download from the website at **eCommerceMasterPlan.com/Free**

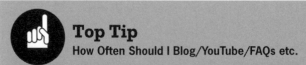

Top Tip
How Often Should I Blog/YouTube/FAQs etc.

Ah, if I had a penny for every time I've been asked…

Well, I'm afraid it's a question with no answer as what's right for one business isn't right for another. But I can give you some guidance:

- There are very few businesses where it's not worth blogging weekly.
- You need to be generating a lot of traffic for it to be worth blogging daily.
- If you don't have something to say – don't blog it.

Generally, the more complex/long the content the less frequently you should produce it. Tweets – several a day is fine, they're only 140 characters. A 30 minute video guide to your products – once a season is fine.

So think of some easy content formats – which are very easy and quick to create and bring a lot of value to the audience. E.g. product of the month, tip of the week etc.

Finally, don't be afraid to repurpose content – a FAQ can become a blog, can become some tweets. A customer competition can become many things.

Get going!

Now you have built your content marketing plan, you need to implement it. So make sure everyone who needs to be creating the content is ready and understands their deadlines, the sign off process and how new content ideas should be raised.

Don't think that you need to be able to do all of this in-house. There are great copywriting services out there that will quickly learn your tone of voice and pull together your blog posts and other content for you. It's well worth investigating this.

Don't forget to look back after a couple of months to see what's working - do more of that and less of what isn't!

. . . .

When Doesn't Content Marketing Work?

Content marketing will have a positive effect for any business; but that doesn't mean it's always worth doing. You have to invest a lot of time (and often money, too) getting your content created and distributed.

So will content bring you enough benefit (sales) to be worth it?

There's no easy way to answer that question because there are thousands of variables, but there are some circumstances in which content is less likely to be effective for your business:

- Regulated marketplaces – if you are selling regulated products, like pharmaceuticals or insurance, there are many restrictions on what you can say about your products. This means it's going to be harder to come up with ideas, and that the creation process will be more expensive because you have to get everything checked by compliance.

- Cheap commodity products – like toothpaste, bottled water, pencils. These are products that people just want to buy; they are cheap enough that it's not worth shopping around, and they don't need extra information on them. People aren't going to be interested in consuming the content, if it's not being consumed it's not worth creating. To succeed with content here, you either need a very exciting idea or you need to spend a lot on building the momentum.

What to Measure in Content Marketing

It's all about consumption of the content – on your site or elsewhere (you usually do get the metrics, wherever you're putting the content).

ENTRY	VISITS	BOUNCE RATE	ORDERS	VALUE	AOV	CONVERSION	SALES/VISIT
Blog post 1	5,000	30%	26	1,820	70	5%	36.4p
Video A	5,000	35%	35	1,575	45	8%	31.5p

You can use this to look at a whole channel – or channels.

As we discussed in the Objectives section at the start of this chapter, it's very hard to separate out the impact of your content from your social media, or search, or other marketing activity. So we have to be a bit clever in the way we measure it. The table above is a simple way to measure the effectiveness of individual pieces of content (Video A vs. Blog B) or channels (YouTube vs. Flickr) by tracking results in analytics at the point where people entered the website, rather than how they got there. The big picture for the content, though, is how well the whole marketing plan functions.

Below are the key metrics to measure for your content marketing; most are in the table above:

- Visits
- Bounce Rate
- Orders
- Conversion Rate
- Sales
- AOV
- Sales per Visitor
- Email sign-up

For more information on each of these metrics see Chapter 10.

. . . .

Successful Content Marketing Checklist:

- What content do you have already?
- What content could you produce/should you produce?
- One idea does not mean one piece of content.
- Choose the right mediums – video, text, and image.
- Create a content creation calendar – and stick to it!
- Track what content works best, and do more of that.
- Get customers to create your content too.

NOTES

What are the key points from this chapter?

_____

_____

_____

_____

_____

_____

_____

_____

_____

_____

_____

_____

_____

_____

WEBSITE
Visit **eCommerceMasterPlan.com** for the latest information on content marketing and more examples of how content marketing could work for you.

CHAPTER 2

Email Marketing

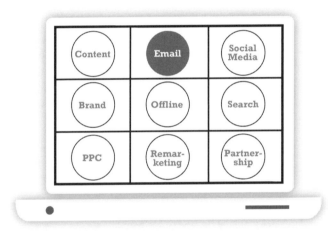

Email marketing is a fantastic way to keep your customers buying and convert your enquirers to buyers.

As soon as you have a list, you can start using some very cheap and good-quality software to email your customers. To really maximise its potential, invest in CRM (customer relationship management) integrated software with which you can drive the right message to the right person at the right time.

GRADUATES

This method is particularly useful for these **eCommerce Business Structures**:

- Online Only
- Mail Order
- Big Bricks and Clicks
- Boutique Bricks and Clicks
- Niche PiggyBack
- Full Multichannel

It works equally well at all positions on the **Product Range Scale**.

It is also particularly useful if your **USP** is:

- Knowledge and Information – because it's a great way to show how much you know.
- Customer Base – email is a powerful way to keep your customer base active, and the larger your customer base, the more effective email can become through segmentation.

Why Should You Use Email if You Are an eCommerce Business?

Email marketing is one of the most effective ways to make money in eCommerce marketing. It's powerful because:

- You get the results almost instantly – people will buy within minutes of the email launching.
- You are in total control – you are in control of the products, promotions, and stories you are putting in front of people, and you are in control of when it goes out and which customers get the message. This means you have a lot of influence over what the outcomes are; which products get bought, how much you sell, and more.
- You can target specific customer groups, getting lapsed customers to buy again or enquirers to buy.
- It should always be profitable – there are so many levels of technology that you should always be able to find a good software solution at a price that means you are making money.

....

Email Marketing Objectives for eCommerce Businesses

Email activity should be focused on hitting your big objectives. Right from the first email you send. It needs to be:

- driving the sales
- keeping your customers active, getting them to buy again and again

As you grow the list size and complexity of your email activity, you can also focus campaigns on increasing AOV, activating enquirers, and much much more.

How Email Marketing Works

The job of every email you launch is to get the customer to the website, as quickly as possible.

If they don't click to the website, they can't buy.

The faster they get to the website, the more likely they are to buy.

WORKBOOK
Download the Email Marketing Workbook from the website at
eCommerceMasterPlan.com/Free

There are several elements that you control in email marketing and each has an impact on the performance of your campaigns:

- Software and hosting – Gets email into the inbox (p. 34)
- From name – Builds trust and recognition (p. 37)
- Subject line – Gets the email opened (p. 38)
- Content and structure – Gets the customer to the website (p. 39)
- Story/Message – Defines how powerful the email will be (p. 42)
- Segmentation – Defines which customer gets which email (p. 42)

You need to get the first four correct for every email you send; they form the bedrock of your email performance and, if they are not right, your email marketing will not drive the volume of sales it should.

The real power though is in the story and the segmentation.

- The **story** is what the whole email (or series of emails) is about: it might be Sale, it might be Spring Collection, it might be Time to Stock up the Bird Table. A strong story, delivered well, will really increase sales.

- The **segmentation** is making sure each customer hears the right story.

The best email result I ever achieved was when we identified customers who had previously bought similar items, and sent them an email specifically about a new range of those items. The email only went to about 1,500 customers, but the Return on Investment (ROI) was off the scale. This was a niche product, so segmenting the 1,500 customers off to receive their own message meant we could send the rest of the database (80,000) a more general message, thus getting a better response from them than we'd have got if we'd sent the niche message to everyone.

Of course, we also had the software, hosting, from name, subject line, and content and structure correct – which all helped, but it was getting the story and segmentation perfect that made the performance so strong.

Top Tip
Email Deliverability

All your effort in email marketing is wasted if you don't get your emails into the inbox; this is called email deliverability and is not the same as the percentage delivered reports you get from your email sending system. Ensuring this happens is hard.

In the offline world:

- A business gets the Royal Mail to deliver their communications to a number of recipients.
- The Royal Mail aims to deliver every piece of communication for the business.

- The recipient deals with the piece of communication as follows: responds/stores/puts in the bin/ignores/contacts the business in order to be removed from future communications.

In the online world:

- The business uses an email service provider (ESP) which provides the IP (black box) to deliver their communications to a number of consumers. (ESPs include Constant Contact, Mail Chimp, Adestra, Infusionsoft etc.)
- The communications sent from the black box are delivered to a number of ISPs (the bit after the @ sign: could be hotmail.com, gmail.com, myfunsite.com, etc.).
- Each ISP checks the communication and decides if they want to deliver it to their users. The checks include:
  - Looking at the content:
    - How much image is there compared to text?
    - Is it information our users want to receive?
  - Looking at the black box, where the email has come from: do we trust this sender?
    - Do other ESPs trust this sender?
    - How have our users previously reacted to communications from this sender?
- Once the ISP has run all their checks, they do one of the following with it:
  - Deliver it to the recipient's inbox
  - Deliver it to the recipient's spam folder
  - Bin it and do not deliver it

- If the ISP decides to deliver; the recipient may interact with their emails via a number of tools. If they use the web service of their ISP (e.g. they log into Hotmail), there are no more steps for the email to go through. If they use other software to interact with their emails, such as Outlook or Thunderbird, the software will run its own set of checks on the email and decide what to do with the email: inbox or junk folder.
- If the recipient receives the piece of communication, they will deal with it as follows:
  - Respond
  - Store
  - Delete
  - Click the unsubscribe link in the email to let the business know they don't want to receive any more emails
  - Click the "SPAM" link provided by the ISP to tell the ISP they don't want to receive any more emails from the business (if too many do this, none of your emails will be delivered by that ISP)

Email deliverability is vital to the success of your campaign. Your potential customers need to be able to see your email in order to make a purchase. Maintaining this deliverability is down to two things: the ESP (the software and hosting) you choose and what email addresses you send to.

So choose your ESP wisely and only email people who want to hear from you.

If you want to go all out on maximising your deliverability, there are two further things you can do: set up the SPF records on your domain and get into white lists.

A **white list** guarantees you are put into the inbox of your customers. The best white list is Return Path's SenderScore Certified. It's not cheap, but if you have a large list it may well be worth it. The criteria for entry are a series of standards you need to meet and adhere to, and they are set pretty high, so becoming compliant may take some time, too.

www.returnpath.com/solution-content/return-path-certification/

SPF is the **Sender Policy Framework**, a way to define where your legitimate emails are sent from. Not all ISPs check this, so it's not critical, but it's free and worth doing if you can.

The SPF record is a text file that sits on your domain's name servers (the same place you go to change your A records and CNAME records). It's pretty simple to get an SPF record in place; more complex to do it right.

If you are going to set up an SPF record, you need to make sure you have included EVERY location that sends email on your domain's behalf. In a typical eCommerce business, these might include:

- Your ESP for your email marketing
- Your Order Management System for your order despatch confirmations
- Your website for your order-placed emails
- Your head office if you use the same URL for your emails
- Your customer service team if outsourcing

If you leave one of them out, the emails sent from that location may well not be delivered because your SPF record will say it's not a legitimate email.

Steps to setting up your SPF:

- Identify everywhere your emails are sent from
- Go to www.openspf.org to find out how to set up the text file
- Put it in place
- Check every location's emails are still working correctly

If any systems change, don't forget to update the SPF record!

Cold emailing is not worth the effort

- Response rates are low and prices are high, so you are unlikely to recruit new customers cost-effectively.
- Data quality is poor – if you go for the cheap lists you are going to get bad data and mailing to that is a waste of your time.
- You could mess up your emailing to your own list (your deliverability), if you mail some cold data and three people on Hotmail hit the "spam" button, you might not get any emails to people using Hotmail for months. That could prove to be very expensive (see Tip Box).

If you do decide you want to do some cold emailing, there are a handful of routes that may be worth testing. The most important thing is not to use the same software that you use to send your normal emails; that way the performance of your house file is protected. You should have a separate email service provider for this, or get the data from someone who will manage the launch for you.

Appending

You use an appending service to find the email addresses of customers you don't have an email address for. The process is usually that the appending company will take your customer database and match it with theirs, then contact your customers to see if they are happy to sign up for your emails. The good thing is that once you have got the data to use, it is opted in so the response should be good. But, it isn't a cheap service; the price reflects the complexity.

Surveys

There are many companies who will run a survey on your behalf to help you collect data. Those filling in the survey will be asked questions agreed to by you and have the opportunity to sign up to your emails. You then get the email addresses of those who wanted to sign up.

You can gather volume quite quickly, but the quality is not always great. Those filling in the surveys are often habitual survey respondents signing up to lots of companies. The questions in the survey help you work out which data you actually want to buy; so if you sell women's clothes, you don't want to buy the men's data. That is fine, but the company running the survey only gets paid for the data you take, so expect them to encourage you to keep the questions pretty generic so there's lots of data for you to buy.

Partnering/buying space in someone else's email

This means paying another company to promote you in their emails. In some cases, you will be able to swap a promotion rather than pay for one (see Chapter 9). As with all partnering, make sure you are both after similar customer types.

Email recruitment

Buying email data doesn't work, so what can we do to increase the list?

The first thing to do is to make sure you are **always asking** for an email address.

Secondly, make sure it's easy for customers to give you their email addresses. Check through all the points where you interact with the customers: where can you improve email address capture? This includes stores and catalogues as well as websites, social media, etc.

Thirdly, make sure your email sign-up is obvious and compelling. Put it somewhere it's going to be seen, and make it easy to use (so ask for as little information as possible). Then test different incentives: prize draws, free downloads, free gifts – see what works best for your business.

Finally, think of where else your customers might be. What magazine or websites do they like? And would those magazines or websites be interested in running a competition for their readers? If they are, you could provide the prize and set up the entry form so that everyone who enters signs up to your emails.

When you are measuring the effectiveness of these recruitment methods, don't just look at how many email addresses you get. Keep the data from each recruitment campaign separate and see how it responds; you want good data not just any data, so the campaign that brought you data that buys is the one you want to do again.

Software and hosting

It's critical to choose the right method of launching your emails. Which ESP you choose will have a major impact on the performance of your email marketing. This is because the quality of your ESP determines whether or not you make it to your customer's inbox or get put into their junk box, or not delivered at all. ESPs also come in very different price brackets, so you need to choose the one that fits your needs and budget now. The good thing is that your need for more complex functionality is driven by the size of your list, which also drives your sales volume; so your sales should grow as your costs grow, meaning email marketing should always have a positive ROI (profit).

Getting into the inbox is based on how companies like Hotmail and Gmail view the black box (IP address) and from address (@email.yourbrand. com) that your email comes from. Their point of view is primarily based on how they have previously seen you and your black box perform: how many times their customers have marked your email as spam; how well their customers respond to your emails (see Deliverability Tip Box). There is a lot you can do to make sure your performance is good:

- Suppress hard bounce notifications.
- Suppress "report as spam" requests from ISPs.
- Suppress inactive data – the "emotionally dormant". If someone hasn't opened any of your emails in over six months, stop sending to them. They have effectively unsubscribed, and these are the people most likely to mark you as spam. Across the lists I have done this on, it has reduced send volumes by over 50%, and has made no impact on sales; it's going to save you money and increase ROI too.
- Monitor performance of all data segments.
- Use multi-part messages (using HTML and text preference fields).
- Have optimal text to image balance.

- Use email layouts that appeal to consumers.
- Have email content/messages relevant to the consumer.
- Double-check emails against spam tools pre-send.
- Have an obvious "unsubscribe" link on the email at the top and bottom, and process them quickly.
- Use a consistent "from name".

If you want to see how you are currently doing then check your SenderScore.

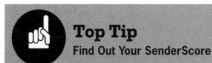

Top Tip
Find Out Your SenderScore

SenderScore is a measure of email deliverability: how many spam filters you will get through. Or (roughly speaking), how likely it is that your emails will get into the inbox. To see how well your emails fare, find out the IP address from which your emails are sent. Either:

- Ask your IT team; OR
- Use Outlook to look at the "internet headers" of a live email. In there is the line "Received: from ... ({111.11.111.11})". The numbers between the brackets are your email sending IP

Once you have your IP address:

- Go to the SenderScore website (www.senderscore.org)
- Enter your IP in the big IP entry box
- Click "Look up"
- On the next page, a number will appear in a big red box – this is your SenderScore. It roughly equates to the percentage of your emails that get into the inbox – you want a score of at least 90%

Why not check out the SenderScore of your competition while you are there?

Selecting your ESP

DOWNLOAD
On the website there is a brief guide to ESPs and
which suit what size of business. You can find it at
eCommerceMasterPlan.com/Free

When you are selecting your ESP, you need to ask these questions:

- What is the cost structure? Monthly fee, set-up costs, price per
  1,000, etc.: price structures vary a lot, so make sure you know
  exactly what you are going to be paying for.
- What is their data policy? What data will they/won't they allow you to
  upload? For some, you sign to agree to the provider's policies and
  others actually put technical blocks in place – to stop you uploading
  info@ email addresses or similar.
- Can they integrate with your systems? Do you need this? If so, what
  are the costs?
- What is their average SenderScore? You need to know how good
  they are at getting your emails to the inbox of your customers.
- Segmentation flexibility. How can you manipulate your data in
  their system? The very simplest may only allow you one list, so no
  segmentation. The most complex allow you to auto-segment and
  build complex mailing plans.
- What will your sending email address be? @yourbrand.com or @
  email.yourbrand.com. Or @theirbrand.com?
- Analytics tracking. Does their system automatically tag all the links in
  your email so you can see the traffic easily in your analytics system
  (e.g. Google Analytics)?
- The help service. How can you get help: by phone, email, forum, or
  online chat?

- How long are you tied in? As your list grows and your business develops, you might want to change ESP. Can you?
- How complex is it to leave? Can you literally just export your HTML and database? Or is it harder than that?

From names

Thankfully, from names are much more straightforward than software and hosting.

Your from name is important because it has a big impact on whether a customer opens your emails. The subject line will be the reason someone opens, but if the from name is wrong, the customer won't get as far as the subject line – they'll just pass over and delete.

The job of the from name is to be recognised and trusted by your customers; it's the constant part of your email marketing.

The from name you should go with will usually be your company name, because that is your brand, which customers have the relationship with. For some businesses, though, it might be the founder's name.

If your product range is quite vast or you email on very different topics, you might want to have a from name that changes a bit. Etsy is a website that has a number of email communication types that customers can sign up to; to make it easy for the customers, each has a different from name:

- Etsy Success – is advice on how to sell more
- Etsy Dudes – is Etsy products for men
- Etsy Finds – is the daily cool-products-found-on-Etsy email
- Etsy Labs – learn from other sellers on Etsy

Choose your from name carefully, and stick with it.

Subject line

The subject line has one job: to get your email opened.

It needs to be either intriguing or obvious:

- Intriguing = "It's All Gone Tribal"
- Obvious = "Sale Now On – Save up to 70%"

Your subject line also needs to attract the right people: those who are going to be interested in the content and buy.

You can find countless blogs and white papers on what does and doesn't work in subject lines. These are useful for one reason and one reason only: to give you some ideas of what you might want to test. There isn't a perfect subject line out there; there is only the best subject line you can use at a given time to advertise a given story to a given data segment.

Start working out some rules for your business; key things to test are:

- Case – Title Case (where the initial letters are all capitals), or Sentence case (where just the first letter is a capital), or lower case (not a capital in sight).
- Include your brand name? It is probably already in the from name.
- Length – long or short? Every subject line should be visible all at once, so you do need to keep it relatively short.
- How obscure can you go?
- Personalisation – does performance improve when you include the recipient's name in the subject line?

If your list is big enough, you can run a test for every email you send; separate out some of the data (at least 10k), split it in half and send each half a different subject line. Twenty-four hours later, send the rest of the data the one that worked best.

If you are going to test subject lines, select your winner based on the performance of the whole email, not just the open rate. We want the right people opening, not just anyone. So look at all the stats.

Sales per delivered is critical – the total sales driven by the email, divided by the number of people the email went to. For example:

LIST	DELIVERED	OPENED	%	CLICKED	%	ORDERS	VALUE	AOV	CONVERSION RATE	SALES/ DELIVERED
A	5,000	1,500	30%	525	35%	26	1,820	70	5%	36.4p
B	8,000	2,800	35%	700	25%	56	2,520	45	8%	31.5p

Even though List B had a higher open rate, List A drove a better return, with a sales per delivered of 36.4p vs. 31.5p. So roll out A.

Content: the body of the email

Once people have opened the email, you want to get them to the website as quickly as possible; ideally within seconds. So design the structure of your email to encourage customers to click. It needs to make it easy for them to click and encourage the click. There are some things that work well in pretty much every eCommerce business's emails:

- Make sure you have some compelling text links at the top of the email: this might be your category headings.
- Preview pane text – that's a line of text repeating the subject line (or is similar to it) that links directly to the page on the website about the subject. Preview pane text should be at the very top left of the email so that it appears in the preview pane if the customer has this set up.
- Most customers will click on the content at the top or at the bottom, so put your best products there and don't spend too long building up the middle.

- Do include prices of the products you feature, and if they are on sale or on offer show the before price too.
- Make anything that can be linkable a link: prices, product name, images, all of it.

Text is good in emails because not everyone downloads the images. If you can get them to click before they have downloaded the images, that's a good thing. Having a good balance between text and images can also help get your emails delivered.

For every marketing email you send, create a text version and an HTML version; it should be obvious how to do this within your ESP's software, so make sure you do it. It improves both deliverability and response. Often, once you have the HTML built, you can automatically create the text version – so it's not that hard to do either!

There are a few things that are good/legally essential to include in every email you send; this is the content you put "above" and "below" the email.

PUT AT THE TOP	PUT AT THE BOTTOM
Preview Pane Text (see above)	Unsubscribe
Add us to your safe senders list	What email address the email was sent to
If you can't see the images click here (with a link to an online version of the email)	If you are a UK limited company, your registered name, address, company number, and the region you are registered under
Link to a mobile version (the text version)	Terms and Conditions for any promotion or competition if required
	Customer service contact details
	Links to your social media profiles

DOWNLOAD
We have copy and paste examples on the website at
eCommerceMasterPlan.com/Free

Once you believe you have a good email design ready to send, you need to check how it renders – this means how it looks in different email systems and mobile handsets. Your email is just some HTML coding that pulls words, images, and links together in a certain way, and that HTML is open to interpretation. The different email systems will interpret it in different ways, so you need to know how well it is being interpreted before you send it to your customers.

To do this, set up an account with each of the systems (Hotmail, Outlook) your customers use to receive your emails and send a test version of your email to each of the accounts. Go and see how it looks, make sure you view it both with and without the images downloaded, and when you are checking it you want to look out for the following things:

- Does it look how I want it to?
- Is it obvious what the customer needs to do next?
- How did the subject line look – was it too long?

Then change your email HTML however you need to and re-test the rendering until you are happy.

WEBSITE
On **eCommerceMasterPlan.com** you'll find a list of key email services to create accounts with.

Story/Message

In your email marketing, there should be a flow of stories defined by your marketing promotions calendar (see *eCommerce MasterPlan 1.8: Your 3 Steps to Successful Online Selling*). Some may be simple one-offs like "New Season Online", or "20% Off Beach Toys"; others will be a more complex series of emails like the Christmas Campaign, or Sale.

Email marketing success comes from how well your stories flow through the year, and how well each email explains its story. The story impacts on the subject line, the content, the data selection and possibly even the from name (e.g. "Your Brand Sale").

As counter-intuitive as it sounds, not all your emails should be trying to sell, especially true if you are building your eCommerce business on a USP of knowledge and information or brand. Some of your emails should be purely about news or knowledge (not that they can't feature products, but the main message shouldn't be about the products), so it might be about a room a customer has created with your paints, or your clothes being worn by a key celebrity. These softer emails build up a better relationship with your customers; they make them warm to your business more and trust you more.

Of course, there is no reason why you shouldn't have an element of this in every email you send, but try sending just one non-sales email each quarter.

Segmentation

Segmentation is where email marketing gets really exciting: what messages do you send to which customers, when?

You should use your segmentation to monitor performance and to push for a better response. Every email you send should be tracked for the response it gets from each of your customer segments. You always want to know how the enquirers responded compared with how the buyers did. How did the lapsed buyers respond vs. those who bought last month? Then, even if you are just sending the same message to everyone, you can start to see how different groups behave so you know how to change things next year to increase the performance further.

Using segmentation to improve results is usually focused on campaigns designed to change customer behaviour for the better, for example:

- Welcome programmes – to either convince enquirers to make the first purchase or encourage first-time buyers to make the second
- Reactivation programmes – to get customers who haven't bought in a while to buy again

These programmes are great ways to increase the business's performance, but what's even better about them is that once you have them working, you can automate them.

Automating elements of your email marketing is powerful and efficient: you just set it up once and it works in the background, keeping the sales coming in. Not all email systems can cope with automation, so make sure you find out what you can do before you start planning.

. . . .

When Doesn't Email Marketing Work?

Email marketing doesn't work if you don't have data. If you don't have an email database, you need to start building one.

I'd like to be able to put here that it doesn't work if you abuse it. And certainly if you over-mail, the response will drop off, but it will take months for it to become ineffective.

. . . .

What to Measure in Email Marketing

From day one, email is all about the money. But to get the most out of it, you also need to track open and click rates to improve response further.

Subject Line	Delivered	Opened	%	Clicked	%	Orders	Value	AOV	Conversion Rate	Sales/ Delivered
A	5,000	1,500	30%	525	35%	26	1,820	70	5%	36.4p
B	5,000	1,750	35%	438	25%	35	1,575	45	8%	31.5p

Below are the key metrics you need to be measuring for your email marketing; most of them are in the table above:

- Attempted
- Delivered
- Delivery rate
- Opened
- Open rate
- Clicked
- Click rate
- Orders
- Conversion rate
- Sales
- AOV
- Sales per delivered

- Unsubscribes
- Unsubscribe rate

For more information on each of these metrics, see Chapter 10.

If you can, it's also good to monitor the number of spam complaints you get. Plus, if you are tracking the email traffic into your Analytics system, then every three to six months have a look at how the traffic is performing: how does its behaviour differ from that of your other traffic sources?

Successful Email Marketing Checklist

- Are you on the right software? Is your ESP doing a good job for you?
- Can you set up an SPF record?
- Select your from name and stick with it.
- Test subject lines to create your rules.
- Construct a great set of stories to tell.
- Tell the story well in every email.
- Get your email content structure right.
- Think about how to grow your list.
- Build your email reporting dashboard and keep looking at it.

NOTES

What are the key points from this chapter?

_____

_____

_____

_____

_____

_____

_____

_____

_____

_____

_____

WEBSITE
Visit **eCommerceMasterPlan.com** for the latest information on email marketing.

CHAPTER 3

Social Media Marketing

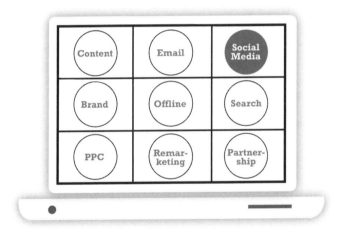

Social media is now part of life; it's part of TV, events, sport, and shopping. It's very hard to ignore.

For eCommerce businesses, it provides a fantastic opportunity for conversations with your customers. Conversations that increase customer loyalty and recommendations, PLUS conversations that help you get more traffic from search engines.

Although social media is everywhere, it is still a very new medium. The big challenges (the ones I'm asked about again and again) are where to start and what to do. In this chapter we're going to explore just that! Focusing on what you need to consider and how to get started – it is not "how to do Twitter" or "how to do Google+".

Available on Amazon Kindle are a number of ebooks I've written about exactly what to do on each platform. There is also another book in this series, *eCommerce Social Media*. Find out more at **eCommerceMasterPlan.com/Books**

GRADUATES

This method is particularly useful for these **eCommerce Business Structures**:

- Online Only
- Boutique Bricks and Clicks
- Niche PiggyBack

Social media works for all points on the **Product Range Scale**.

It is also particularly useful if your **USPs** are:

- Knowledge and Information – because it's a great way to show how much you know.
- Customer Service – because different customers like to contact you in different ways – so you need to be there when they want to contact you.

Why Should You Use Social Media if You Are an eCommerce Business?

Social media marketing has an impact beyond just sales driven by social media; there are lots of reasons to use it:

- Customers now have lots of different ways to interact; they are the ones choosing how they want to be communicated with, not the other way around. So if your customers want to communicate with you on Twitter, you should join in.
- It's a powerful way to prove how well you know your area, to prove your expertise.
- Everything you do on social media will help improve your search marketing traffic, too.

But, don't do it unless you want to talk to and communicate with your customers; if you try to manipulate social media just for search marketing, it won't work nearly as well as if you put the same effort into doing it "properly". Don't do it unless you have some content to talk about.

WEBSITE
Find our latest social media glossary at
eCommerceMasterPlan.com/Free

Social Media Marketing Objectives for eCommerce Businesses

Like all marketing for eCommerce, social media activity needs to bring in the sales, so although it will take a few months (or more) to build up a big enough follower base to get noticeable sales, you should track the results from day one. You also need objectives for follower growth and the level of engagement you're getting.

Finally, you need to be consistent – so objectives for activity are also going to be valuable.

. . . .

How Social Media Marketing Works

Social media is "a group of internet-based applications that … allow the creation and exchange of user-generated content."

I like this definition because it's so simple and using social media is simple. It's just about communicating with like-minded people about things that interest you. Assuming you are interested in the products you sell and that your customers and potential customers are also interested in those products, it should be easy. Shouldn't it?

The three reasons for not using social media that I hear most frequently from eCommerce businesses are:

- We don't have anything to say.

- We don't have the time to do it.
- What if customers complain to us on social media?

We are going to address all of these as we go through this section, but before we get into the nitty-gritty, I want to explain the core social media strategy for eCommerce.

No matter which social media platform you choose to use (Facebook, Twitter, Google+, Pinterest, or whatever launches next year) to be successful you need to grow your **followers** and their **engagement** with you, so your fundamental approach should remain the same:

- Tell your existing customers that you are on social media so they can follow you there – to build your follower base and get traffic to your website.
- Follow others interested in the same topics – to build your follower base and get traffic to your website.
- Share content – to start conversations.
- Engage in discussions – to build your follower base and get traffic to your website.

Getting great results from social media relies on your shares (or shares about you) being **engaged with**. When shares are engaged with (liked, commented on, retweeted, repinned etc.), they'll be seen by more people. Plus, on some social networks (notably Facebook), the more you are engaged with, the more people will see <u>all</u> your shares.

But to get started, you don't have to dive in with both feet. Yes, go and register all your companies on all social media platforms to make sure you have your name when you want it, but don't think you have to start using them all straight away. The other great thing about social media is that you can let others do the hard work for you by getting your **on-site social media** in place. This means:

- Integrate social sharing buttons on the website – to get your website visitors doing the hard work by sharing your content on social media for you (see Tip Box p. 66).

....

How to Create Your Social Media Plan

WORKBOOK
To help you through this section, go to **eCommerceMasterPlan.com/Free** and download our Social Media Workbook.

There are five stages to creating a social media plan:

- Know your audience
- Avoid the pitfalls
- Plan your strategy
- Choose your tools
- Get going!

Stage 1: Know your audience

The very first thing you need to research is what your audience are already doing on social media. Your audience is your customers, your potential customers and those talking about products like yours. They are the people you are going to want to be communicating with on social media. To understand what they are doing on social media is not that hard, it just requires a bit of time investigating.

First, look at your analytics. Do you already have traffic coming to your website from social media tools? If so, where from and how does that traffic behave?

Use the traffic sources data in Google Analytics and do a filter search for each of the social media platforms (change the date range to the last 12 months):

- Twitter
- t.co (also Twitter)
- Facebook
- Pinterest
- LinkedIn
- Plus.Google
- Others you think may be relevant

If you are getting lots of visits from Twitter, then that would be a good platform to start on! If there is quite a bit of traffic, you will also be able to see which pages of the website are being linked to – that will give you an idea of what content your audience are already sharing on social media.

Secondly, take a look on the social media platforms themselves to see how much discussion is already going on in your area. This is not as difficult as it sounds.

Identify some keywords to search for. They should be important keywords for your business or those that describe where/when your products are used, e.g. if you sell wallpaper, search "interior design". These might include:

- your brand name
- keywords that describe your sector
- product names and category names
- your competitors

Just go to each platform and search on those keywords; you'll soon find out if there are conversations already happening, what topics they are on and who's talking about them. These are people you'll want to be connecting with.

Summarise this in a table:

	Visitors Last 12m	Sales Last 12m	Conversation Volume 1-10	Conversation Quality 1-10	Anyone mentioned us?
Pinterest	1,000	£750	6	6	Y
Twitter	500	£100	4	2	Y
Facebook	200	£150	2	2	N

DOWNLOAD
You can download a version of this table from
eCommerceMasterPlan.com/Free

If there is nothing, think long and hard about your product on social media. Did you pick the wrong keywords? Is it a new area that you believe will work?

Stage 2: Avoid the pitfalls

Now you know you want to do social media and which platforms you're going to use, you need to be prepared for things going wrong. A lot can go wrong in social media and it happens quickly, here are some examples of when it goes wrong:

On the 5th February 2010, one of Vodafone UK's customer service team tweeted on @VodafoneUK:

This was a one-off error, probably caused by someone accidentally tweeting via the company's Twitter account rather than their personal account.

The retailer Kenneth Cole couldn't use that excuse in February 2011, when it used #Cairo (being used for the uprisings) to promote their new spring collection, even customising the short URL to include Cairo! They meant to do it, just didn't realise it was a bad idea.

The impact was huge; these messages got retweeted and spread like wildfire through the internet. With social media, you don't have control over your content. You won't find any of these tweets on the accounts they were originally tweeted on – all were deleted. But they had already been retweeted, so the content was unstoppable. Don't think this is restricted to Twitter – it can happen on any platform. Although these errors spread very far, very fast, they die out quite quickly when apologies are swiftly issued.

These examples highlight the inherent danger of social media communication. Messages are short, conversations need to flow and activity is done quickly. You can't proof every social media message like you would an advertising campaign.

If you can't proof everything, how can you minimise the chances of this happening in your business? You need to put in place guidelines and training, which is all part of your social media corporate guidelines, they should include:

- A disaster recovery plan – how will you deal with an issue such as the above if it happens? Deleting the content, issuing an apology, investigating quickly and dealing with the cause of the problem.
- A social media HR policy, to enable you to take swift action when necessary.
- A social media usage policy – that everyone is familiar with and follows. This needs to be simple and easy to understand, but still cover the basics like "do not use personal social media accounts at the same time as the company account". (See the Top Tip below for some examples.)
- Training – train the team both on how to use the tools and platforms and how social media works – including your usage policy.

Top Tip
Social Media Usage Policies

Social media usage policies come in *many* shapes and sizes. Here are some examples:

Zappos.com – simply state: be real and use your best judgement

eConsultancy – have two versions: the short (be nice, don't tell lies, don't feed the trolls) and the full version, which is:

- Listen closely. That's what your ears are for.
- Respond to questions/queries/concerns in a timely fashion.
- When you respond, remember that you are a human, not a "'PRbot". A little personality is more than OK.
- Have a thick skin and take all criticism on the chin (but stick up for yourself where necessary).
- Learn the difference between cheekiness and spamminess. Kiss the former, kill the latter.
- Coordination and consistency (of messaging) is important. Talk among yourselves.
- Raise flags internally, as and when appropriate.
- Denial, wool-pulling and hole-digging is bad. Admitting mistakes and saying sorry is good (relatively speaking).
- Always pause for a moment in private before you reply in public.
- Be responsible.

IBM states:

- Don't pick fights; be the first to correct your own mistakes and don't alter previous posts without indicating that you have done so.

- Try to add value. Provide worthwhile information and perspective. IBM's brand is best represented by its people, and what you publish may reflect on IBM's brand.
- Speak in the first person. Use your own voice. Bring your own personality to the forefront. Say what is on your mind.

INTEL advises:

- Always pause and think before posting.
- Perception is reality.
- It is a conversation.

(originally published by eConsultancy.com)

Stage 3: Plan your strategy

Now you have your corporate social media policy and know where your audience is, you need to build up the plan and decide what you're actually going to do!

There are two parts to the activity plan. The first is to decide how social media will be promoted by the rest of your marketing and the second is to work out what you are going to be talking about and who is going to be talking about it.

Promoting within your existing marketing

Put simply, you are going to put links to your social media activity on all your customer touch points.

With your online marketing, add active buttons wherever you can in offline marketing activities. Include "Find us on ..." text and logos that make it easy for people to find and follow you on social media.

Active buttons are buttons that don't just link someone to your social media pages; when clicked on, that person (if they are logged into their social media profile) will be added as a follower. You can download these buttons from each platform then get your website builder or email coder to add each piece of code to your online marketing. Or you can use a tool like AddThis, which will give you one piece of code that will add all your social media buttons. Active buttons come in lots of shapes and sizes, so have a look at what is available and implement the right one for you. Just make sure you put it in place, as it's a great way to increase your followers.

This is pretty much a one-off task; once in place you don't need to worry too much about it. Your communications are where you are going to be spending your time and effort.

Building the activity plan

Firstly, you need to work out what content you have already got that you can share on social media. This is the process that was detailed in Chapter 1 when we were creating our content marketing plans. The content you have on your website will be at the heart of your social media activity, not least because your end goal is to get people to the website and to buy. To this, you should add the information you found when researching what your audience was talking about already on social media. This is what you will tweet/post/share/pin on your social media platforms.

On top of this, though, you want to be interacting with people. This interaction will be in the form of conversations you start and conversations you join. This activity will build engagement, and engagement is what will drive traffic to you. Finding conversations to join in is pretty easy (there is more on this below) and so is creating conversations!

Sharing the content from the website will create some conversations, but you want to be more proactive than that. You need to create social media campaigns to generate more.

A social media campaign is a series of communications on the same topic which aim to provoke debate. They can be very simple, such as "Top 10 British Authors", or very complex, such as "Design the cover of our new catalogue to win one of everything in it".

WEBSITE
You can find lots of examples of great social media campaigns on the website **eCommerceMasterPlan.com**

Initially you should be aiming for a campaign at least every month and try different types of campaign. Then you will learn quickly what works best; what gets the most engagement. The campaigns can run across all your social media, or just one platform. The best campaigns are ones that create new campaigns; so you might do a campaign that's a survey or poll, then you can publish the results (providing content and PR) and ask for comments on the results and 12 months later you can re-run it to see what has changed.

Here are some ideas:

- Top 10
- Our customers' favourites
- Voted for by you

- Top tips
- Predicted best sellers
- New trends
- Competitions
- Surveys

 WEBSITE
You'll find more ideas at **eCommerceMasterPlan.com/ Free**

Once you have your ideas, it's time to add them to your promotional calendar and fit them in with all your other marketing activity.

Stage 4: Choose your tools

Now you should have LOADS of ideas for what you want to do in your social media and be itching to get going.

Before you can do that, though, you need to choose which social media platforms you are going to start with and the tools you are going to use to make your social media activity **efficient and effective**.

Social media platform choice

There are hundreds of social media platforms, from Facebook and Twitter to Pinterest and StumbleUpon. You need to choose which you are going to use and when – you don't have to start them all at once. The research we did in Stage 1 (into where your audience is) should make that decision pretty easy, but you also need to bear in mind how popular each platform is. As I'm writing this, Twitter and Facebook are big and well established, but Google+ and Pinterest are gaining ground fast.

You may decide that you want to at least establish a profile on several sites, but concentrate your efforts on one initially; that can be a great way to go as you will get real feedback on how quickly each grows for you and redeploy your resources accordingly.

WEBSITE
You will find up-to-date statistics on each of the main social media platforms on the website **eCommerceMasterPlan. com/Free** to help you make your decision.

Tools to be effective and efficient

Now you know what platforms you are going to use, you are almost ready to start. But we need to get the tools in place that are going to make your social media activity efficient and effective; to put it simply, save you time and enable you to do more.

This is the secret of social media. As we worked through the content, you were probably thinking "This is going to take me hours, every week!" or "I know I'm going to forget to do it some days". Well, it's not going to take you as much time as you think and it doesn't matter if you forget some days.

There are thousands of tools out there that will help you manage your social media activity and help you do things like:

- Schedule the activity, so you can set up all the communication for your campaign in one go.
- Find people to follow who are interested in the same things as you.
- Run competitions.
- Encourage email sign-ups.
- Automatically post content as you create it – yes, your blog posts can be set up to be posted automatically onto all your social media. The same can be done with images and videos, too.

- Run your keyword searches.
- Let you know when there is something you need to respond to.
- Reporting.

Plus there are lots of options for each one: some are free, some you pay for, but spending a little time now finding the right ones for you and putting them in place will save you lots of time later and make all your effort more effective.

By automating some content, you can afford to forget one day, because communications will happen without you. By scheduling a campaign in one go, it will be more cohesive and therefore more powerful.

At the centre of all this, you need a great social media management tool; there are several options out there. My favourite is Hootsuite. It enables me to:

- manage all my social media platforms in one place
- see what's happening on them
- post to all of them in one go (yes, one update – all platforms!)
- monitor keywords I'm interested in
- schedule future updates

Not all conversations you want to be part of will come to you: you also need to go out and find conversations to join. When researching the audience, you identified a number of keywords to search on: these are your starting point. On your social media management tool (Hootsuite) set each keyword up as a saved search. Every day or so (depending on the volume of content), you should be checking these searches to find conversations to join in with. Look out especially for people who are already talking about you!

WEBSITE
On the website you will find mind maps of the key tools available for the social media platforms.
eCommerceMasterPlan.com/Free

Stage 5: Get going!

You should now have a pretty solid social media plan, have the right tools in place and know how you're going to deal with any issues that crop up, so you can start your activity.

Don't forget to check the results and change your strategy as you need to; there are always things changing in social media, so you need to be ready to drop tactics that aren't working anymore and embrace new opportunities.

Top Tip
Tracking Social Media Traffic to Your Website

The traffic sent to your website by social media will be reported in your analytics as various sources. Some will be simply from the URL of the tool (e.g. Twitter.com) and some will come in tagged as the tool you are using (e.g. Twitter/Twitterfeed). This makes reporting on the impact of social media quite tricky, make sure you are gathering all the sources together. Also, to track the performance of individual campaigns, you may want to tag the links you are putting in that campaign so you can see them in Google Analytics too. (Search "Google URL Builder" to find the tool you need.)

Customer service on social media

Sooner or later your social media activity will attract customer service queries, so you need to be ready for these. Here are a few handy tips to make sure you are prepared:

- Involve the customer service team from the start – make sure they understand how you are going to be using social media and listen to what they think about how customers will respond.
- Make sure they are ready to get involved as soon as you get customer queries coming in. Include them in the training process.
- It is fine to ask a customer on social media to email more details to your customer services so you can deal with the issue more effectively.
- Try to get back to any customer service comments within a few working hours.
- Take a look at your existing customer service response times – if you are not getting back to emails within 24 hours, you are likely to get lots of messages on social media. So try and speed up existing response times so that customers don't have to resort to social media.

One of my clients launched a competition on Facebook but hadn't briefed the store staff, so the first few comments were complaints that they couldn't enter! By including them from the start, you can avoid such embarrassing incidents.

Top Tip
One Piece of Social Media that EVERY eCommerce Business Should Embrace: Share Buttons

Share buttons are the buttons you see on each page of a website that enable visitors to easily share the content on social media.

On an eCommerce site, share buttons should be on every product page, so it becomes really easy for customers to share the great products they are finding on your website with others. This:

- creates social media activity you don't have to start
- starts a conversation to join in – you can thank them for tweeting your products
- helps you get more search traffic (see Chapter 6)

Getting the buttons in place is pretty easy (just like the Like/Follow buttons that get people to like your social media profiles). Either you can go to each social media tool and access their code and put that in place, or you can use a tool like AddThis to gather all the code into one place for you. Then just get it added to the product page template and you are all set.

When Doesn't Social Media Work?

Social media doesn't work if you haven't got anything to say. There is nothing more detrimental to a customer's perception than a dormant, unloved social media profile. So if you are not going to commit to engaging in the conversation, don't start it.

As well as having something to say, in eCommerce you also need to have the customer service team on board; sooner or later you will get customer queries coming through, so make sure you are ready.

There are also a few regulated industries where it's hard to engage in social media because there are huge restrictions on what you can and can't say in your marketing.

What to Measure in Social Media Marketing

There is a wealth of statistics available in social media. I have found the following structure the easiest way to compare performance across channels and keep the data to a manageable level. You need at least one of each of these types of metric for each social media channel you are engaged with:

- **Productivity** A way of tracking the actual impact of your social media activity – sales and website visits. Initially you will find you get very little productivity response to your social media activity, but as your scale and engagement build, you will be able to compare this with previous months and other channels.

- **Engagement** How much your customers engage with you on social media – you'll find this is the number that influences sales. As you grow your social media activity, you will be creating your own set of benchmarks for how you expect engagement to function.
- **Scale** The size of your social media audience – you need some volume here in order to drive enough engagement to drive enough productivity. You want this to keep growing, but only with quality followers – if they are not engaging with you, there is no point in having them.
- **Activity** What did you do? You need to track what you did in order to see how that increases scale and engagement.

	Twitter	Facebook	Pinterest	Google+
Productivity	Visits to your website Sales			
Engagement	Retweets @Mentions Tweets about you	Comments on content Likes of content	Pins of your images Likes of images	+1s of content Comments Hangouts
Scale	Followers	Page Likes	Board Followers	Page Followers
Activity	Number of tweets How many following	Content put up Conversations engaged in	Items pinned Items Liked Conversations engaged in	Content put up Hangouts engaged in Size of circles

Not all the numbers we need are easily available. With a lot of them, you can only get numbers by noting them down on the day, so you need to make sure you keep up to date with compiling your social media performance. For more information on each of these metrics, see Chapter 10.

There are a number of social media reporting tools; some paid, some free. I haven't yet found one at a reasonable price that gives me what I want in my reporting, but as soon as I do find one, I will be writing about it at **eCommerceMasterPlan.com**

Successful Social Media Marketing Checklist

- Have you selected the right social media platforms? (Twitter, Facebook, etc.)
- Have you got your automated activity in place?
- Have you got the tools set up to make it easy for you to run?
- Is the reporting dashboard ready?
- Do you know what you are going to be communicating about for the next few months?
- Is your customer services team ready to go?
- Have you worked out a corporate social media strategy?

WEBSITE

Visit **eCommerceMasterPlan.com** for the latest information on the key social media tools, including case studies of what is working for other eCommerce businesses, and guides on setting up your social media tools.

If you're keen to get your social media really moving fast – then get a copy of the third book in the eCommerce MasterPlan series – *eCommerce Social Media* from **eCommerceMasterPlan.com/Books**

NOTES

What are the key points from this section?

_____

_____

_____

_____

_____

_____

_____

_____

Other Notes:

_____

_____

_____

_____

_____

_____

_____

_____

_____

_____

CHAPTER 4

Brand Awareness Marketing

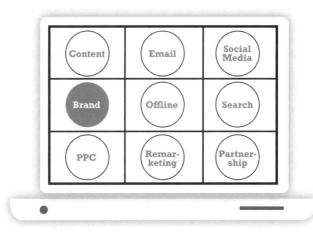

There is some brand awareness in anything you do that's seen by the public – shops, catalogues, social media. But there are also pure brand awareness activities. These are the marketing activities where it's impossible to track sales/response. For example adverts at the front of glossy magazines, or PR.

GRADUATES

This method is particularly useful for these **eCommerce Business Structures**:

- Online Only
- Big Bricks and Clicks
- Niche PiggyBack
- Full Multichannel

Product Range Scale – if you're at the niche end it's easy and at the department-store end you **have** to build it!

It is also particularly useful if your **USP** is:

- Brand – if your USP is your brand, then you **must** build that brand.
- Customer Service – if you are building a reputation for great customer service, that sits very well with building brand awareness.
- Knowledge and Information – this is both a way to build brand awareness and something to base that brand on.

Why Should You Build Brand Awareness if You Are an eCommerce Business?

The more aware a potential customer is of your business, the more likely they are to buy from you. Customer awareness is a way to build trust and that removes a barrier to conversion. If what they know about your business is good, they are far more likely to buy; if what they know about your business is consistent – again, they are far more likely to buy.

Building brand awareness is about making sure your target consumers know about your business AND that the impression they have is the one you want them to have.

- The more aware your target customers are of your brand, the easier it will be to convince them to buy.
- If your customers feel strongly about your brand, they are more likely to forgive you when mistakes happen and it builds loyalty and customer recommendations.

Brand Awareness Objectives for eCommerce Businesses

It is very hard to measure the impact of a brand awareness building activity. This means it is pretty difficult to set objectives.

When I worked at Barclays, brand awareness was measured on a "warmth" scale (from 0–100), so every month a survey was done to see how "warmly" consumers felt about Barclays. Before the bank started actively tracking this warmth scale, a management consultancy had worked out that if "warmth" could be increased by 1 point, it would be the equivalent of several extra £100,000 on the bottom line. Barclays spent a vast sum of money on coming up with the formulas and tracking the results. That is beyond most eCommerce businesses, but it doesn't mean that there shouldn't be brand awareness objectives.

If you get the branding right and consistent across all your marketing, everything should improve (response rates, AOV, customer retention, conversion rate, and more). If, right now, you don't have a strong brand, it will take months (if not years) for you to see the impact of the brand awareness activity.

How Building Brand Awareness Works

Traditionally, brand awareness has been left to the PR department; now it's more complex because there are so many more ways to go about it (from events, to social media, to press, to everything in-between) and because social complaining means you have to live up to what you say your brand is.

To build brand awareness, you need to succeed in three areas:

- Have a clear brand, and know what it stands for
- Consistently deliver that brand
- Do activity "above the parapet" that will put your brand in front of lots of people

In this chapter, we are going to run through each of these in turn.

WORKBOOK
Build your brand more successfully by going to the website and downloading the Brand Awareness Workbook from here:
eCommerceMasterPlan.com/Free

Identifying your brand and what it stands for

Your brand is much more than just a logo. It is the identity that customers and future customers, engage with and believe in. So you want them to trust it and to feel an affinity with it. It should overlap a lot with your USP, as your USP is what your company should pride itself on.

For more on USPs, see the first book in this series *eCommerce MasterPlan*, available at **eCommerceMasterPlan.com/Books**

Whatever stage your business is at, you probably already have a good idea of what your brand is. So this step really is about identifying and outlining the brand that already exists, not creating it.

To identify it, you need to include what everyone in the business thinks it is. So gather the thoughts of your team in answer to the following questions. (You might want to do this via a meeting, an email, or survey, or even an evening down the pub – it depends on the size of your team!)

- What is {company name}?
- What do customers think when they think of {company name}?
- What do we want customers to think of when they think of us?
- Who are we?
- What do we do?
- What do we stand for?

You may also find it useful to ask the same questions of people outside your business: your friends, key suppliers, or customers.

You will get very different answers; but you will also see some real themes emerging. Hopefully the themes are ones you want your brand to stand for; if not, you're going to have to change things before you can get the customer to believe it, and then it's going to be much easier to implement.

Either by yourself, or with your management team, you then need to crystallise the information you have gathered and pull it together into a coherent statement about what the brand is and what it stands for.

Once you have defined what your brand stands for, you can create:

- A logo
- A set of brand guidelines: how can the logo be used, what fonts do you use, colours, etc.?
- A voice/brand statement: what does the brand (your company) stand for? It should be just a page or two of copy.

Consistency: living up to your brand

Now you have your brand clearly outlined, you need to make sure that your whole business reflects that brand; right from the marketing you send out, to the products, to your people and the parcel.

If your brand is about luxury, you need to be sending out your products in quality packaging – not just stuffed in a jiffy bag! If your brand is about the environment, you should be minimising your packaging as much as possible. If you are all about customer service, then why do you not take calls on a Sunday? The more you explore the brand, the more you will realise how important it is to consistently reflect it in everything the business does.

Your brand is only as good as your last interaction with a customer, so everything needs to be on-brand, every time. To truly make that happen, you can't only focus on getting the customer-facing activity on-brand. Everything the business does needs to be on-brand. For example, if you are all about customer service yet your own employees feel like they are treated badly, then you need to improve your HR processes. If you are a luxury brand and your team has to drink cheap instant coffee, you should probably install a good coffee machine.

Follow the process by looking at every touch point the customer has with you: how well does every step line up with the brand? Identify everything you are doing that is not in line with your brand and change it. You will find lots of activities that are not quite as consistent as they could be: these also will need to be improved.

Of course, you can't do all this overnight, so you need to plan how everything is going to be made consistent with the brand. A lot of this will rely on people, so as part of this you must make sure everyone understands the brand, why it is important, and how what they do day to day can affect it.

It is well worth spending time and money on getting everything you do consistent with your brand; this is the activity that will make it obvious what you stand for. It will be obvious what you stand for because it's what you do day in, day out.

Taking your brand above the parapet to build awareness

Simply making your brand consistent in the business will build awareness on its own; staff and customers will talk about the experience they have had and how it appealed to them. Once you are thoroughly living up to your brand, you can take it above the parapet to accelerate how quickly people become aware of your brand and company.

By this point, you are already making your brand clear in all your marketing activity – so there's already quite a bit of brand awareness being built. But there is more you can do to accelerate the process. What you do depends on the brand itself, because what you do needs to fit with it.

If you are all about the lowest prices in vitamins, then hiring a cruise ship for a week for your 100 best customers, suppliers and journalists would be an odd thing to do. Proving you are the best value and running a PR campaign on that wouldn't be an odd thing to do, nor would sponsoring some amateur sports teams, or creating a national vitamin C day.

The aim of any above-the-parapet activity you plan to do is to generate conversations about your business: conversations that reinforce your brand and that people will remember. You need to choose your methods and content carefully; think through any potential issues that might arise from the message getting confused.

Common brand awareness-raising tactics include:

- Press releases and other PR activity
- Blogger liaison – building relationships with influential bloggers in your marketplace
- Social media
- Surveys and opinion polls
- Events – both organised events and flash-mob-style spontaneous events
- Sponsorship
- Creating a "National Day of X"

In common with all marketing, some of these are very cheap while others can be hugely expensive. But with social media now having such an impact on the news, it can be quite easy to come up with simple, effective and cheap ways to build your brand.

It is time for another brainstorm to work out what you should do. Now your team is clear on what the brand stands for and has seen how focusing on it has changed the business, it's time to get together and see what ideas you can come up with – from the big and crazy to the small and simple. Make a note of all the ideas and pick one of the simpler ones to start with!

When Doesn't Building Brand Awareness Work?

Every eCommerce business will benefit from getting brand consistency across their customer interactions. So no eCommerce business should entirely ignore brand awareness, but you should be doing what fits your market and business size. If you are an Etsy seller, going to a craft show or getting featured in an Etsy email are great ideas, but running a billboard campaign less so.

Not all eCommerce businesses will benefit from going beyond that in building brand awareness. Smaller businesses selling price-sensitive products are much less likely to find it worthwhile; so if you are selling commodity electronics, customers are going to buy from you because you've got that specific camera at the best price. Saying that, if you are in that marketplace and you want to get serious growth, then you are going to reach a point where you need to keep customers buying from you and at that point brand awareness will become important.

How to Measure Brand Awareness

Measuring brand awareness is not easy. As we discussed above, it ultimately will be judged a success or not if your sales and overall performance increase.

You should be looking at trends in all statistics you are measuring and those should be improving if your brand awareness is working. In addition, something I have always found useful to do is gather some data via a customer survey. Asking a mix of quantitative and qualitative questions should give you an idea of how customers feel about you. I would run questions similar to the following every six months, collecting the responses of both website visitors and buyers:

- How likely are you to recommend {business name} to others? (On a scale of 1 to 4.)
- If you could change one thing about {business name}, what would it be? (Open response.)
- What is your favourite thing about {business name}? (Open response.)
- From which other stores/websites/catalogues do you buy products like ours? (Initially you will have an open box here, but after the first few surveys you will be able to change that to a series of tick boxes with an "Other" box included.)

The last question is particularly useful because it helps you work out which brands you are up against, so you can look at how they are positioning themselves and make sure you are at least one step ahead.

Once you're doing activity above the parapet, record results in a table like this.

Activity	Impressions	Cost	Cost per 1,000 Impressions	Brand Recall	Sign-ups	Response Rate
Radio	5,000,000	7,000	1.4	51%	3,000	0.06%
Billboards	50,000	5,000	100	10%	500	1.00%
Feature in Magazine	500,000	3,000	6	60%	1,000	0.20%

Key metrics in brand awareness include:

- Impressions
- Cost per 1,000 impressions
- Brand recall
- Sign-ups
- Response rate

For more information on each of these metrics, see Chapter 10.

....

Successful Brand Awareness Checklist

- Really understand the brand you are promoting.
- Make sure everything the business does fits with the brand – everything!
- All promotional activity should fit with the brand too.
- Think about activity you can do to create brand awareness.
- Track the impact on how aware people are of you, but also the impact on bottom-line sales.

NOTES

What are the key points from this section?

_____

_____

_____

_____

_____

_____

Other Notes:

_____

_____

_____

_____

_____

WEBSITE

Visit **eCommerceMasterPlan.com** for more information on how eCommerce businesses are building their brands.

CHAPTER

5

Offline Marketing

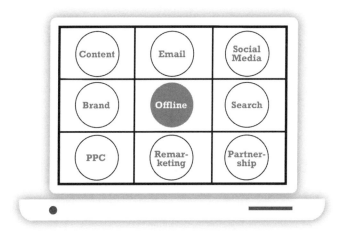

There are lots of overlaps between offline marketing and brand awareness – offline marketing is distinct because it is designed to directly drive conversions, not just increase consumer awareness. Think – catalogues, pop-up shops, trade shows, off-the-page advertising.

GRADUATES

This method is particularly useful for these **eCommerce Business Structures**:

- Mail Order
- Big Bricks and Clicks
- Boutique Bricks and Clicks
- Full Multichannel

Product Range Scale – fine at either end.

It is also particularly useful if your **USP** is:

- Brand – to build a brand you need to build awareness and offline marketing can give you much greater visibility than online alone and should be self-funding.

Why Should You Use Offline Marketing if You Are an eCommerce Business?

Offline marketing is mainly used by eCommerce businesses to provide something they can't get online. Generally, that is scale: getting in front of more people, getting hold of a bigger list, increasing response. So as well as providing something you can't get with online marketing, it is a way to accelerate the growth of your business. Offline marketing has the following benefits:

- The offline marketing industry is a more mature marketplace where there are mapped-out ways to do things. So it can be very straightforward to launch.
- There is more access to volume. We discussed in Chapter 2 that renting email data is a bad idea because good-quality lists don't exist. That is not the case with offline data – there are hundreds of great sources of quality, responsive mailing data that will perform for you.
- Response rates are higher than with online direct marketing.
- Visibility is much greater offline than online – press ads and catalogues hit many more people than online marketing. Print hangs around for longer and gets seen by multiple people.

Offline Marketing Objectives for eCommerce Businesses

Offline marketing activity should be focused on hitting your big objective: sales.

It might not be immediate sales – it might be building your buyer list for future sales; the activity might not be profitable but it must bring in the orders.

Offline marketing (broadly) moves slowly, so it takes longer to optimise. You may be able to optimise your PPC Campaigns within six months, but with postal mailings it will take a year or more to optimise your choice of lists. It also tends to cost a lot more than online marketing (in actual spend, if not in ROI) and as the response comes in slowly, you have to be able to risk more with offline marketing, it might cost £10,000 or more for a campaign and once it's out there, you can't change it.

How Offline Marketing Works

Offline marketing can be many things; here we are going to focus on marketing which happens offline that is intended to directly drive a response, driving customers to visit your website (or shop, or phone you) and order. This broadly falls into three categories:

- **Direct Mail –** you select potential customers to target and mail them something in the post.
- **Shops and Shows –** taking your products to events where you expect your customers to be. They could be a pop-up shop, market stall, or a stand at a show.
- **Advertising –** you target potential customers by putting advertising in places likely to appeal to people like your customers. Usually this would be advertising in newspapers and magazines.

We'll cover each of these in turn.

Direct Mail

Direct Mail is a hugely powerful way to recruit customers and generate sales. Response rates are generally better than with online marketing: usually 1% or higher, even for cold mailings.

WORKBOOK
Download our Direct Mailing Workbook from the website now to help you build your direct mail campaign:
eCommerceMasterPlan.com/Free

A pack for direct mail could be anything from a simple postcard to a several-hundred-page catalogue. Costs and responses differ massively, depending on what format you choose to go with. If you have never done any volume direct mail before, I strongly recommend you get someone involved who has experience in this area as they will be able to improve your performance and save you a lot of money and effort along the way. Direct mail is a very mature tactic, so there are lots of tips and tricks that could save you a fortune.

Once you have decided on your mailing format, you need to start creating your campaign. To have time to get it right, start this at least eight weeks before you want to post it.

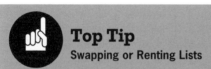

Top Tip
Swapping or Renting Lists

One of the best places to get cold data is from another eCommerce business. Most do rent their data; even better than that is if they are interested in your data and then you can do a swap. They allow you to mail 10,000 of their customers and rather than paying them, you allow them to mail 10,000 of yours.

Data swaps usually start from 10,000 0–12 month buyers, so you need to have had 10,000 people buy from you in the last 12 months who are happy for you to sell their data.

If you are scared that you may lose customers to the other company – well yes, you might. But you may lose them anyway and they may lose customers to you. I know a lot of business owners who have shied away from swaps for exactly that reason; almost all of them are now engaged in swapping data with competitors and wish they had done it years ago.

Find the data

If you don't have anyone to send your mailing to, it's not going to work! Before committing to any other costs, you should make sure you can get enough quality data to make the activity hit your targets.

Every mailing will probably include a mix of data you already have and cold data that you have bought or swapped, so in creating your data plan you should consider the following:

- What data do you already have?
- Would any of your target partners (see Chapter 9) be willing to swap data with you?
- Would any of your target partners be willing to rent you data?
- Speak to a list broker. Explain who you are targeting; they will provide you with a list of suggestions for data you could swap or buy.
- Speak to the data cooperatives. These are businesses who compile vast databases from which they can create a list of the type of customers you want – usually based on geodemographic profiling tools (Abacus, Transactis, etc).

Remember that every mailing should include data testing; even if one of the cold data sources has a possible 100,000 you could mail, don't. Just test 10,000–20,000, then if successful, roll out to the rest in your next mailing.

Once you know you can get the data and how many you are going to be mailing, you can start the design process.

Design it

Depending on the size of the mailing piece, this could be a short or a very long process. Assuming you are going to feature products in the mailing piece, you will need to go through the following stages:

- Selection – choose the products you are going to feature.
- Create an outline – what products on which pages (and other content).
- Photograph all the products.
- Write all the copy.
- Start designing.
- Perform several rounds of proofing before sign-off.
- Then send it to the repro house; they will make sure the colours are right. It is very important when you are aiming to get people to buy products that the products look like they do in the pictures.
- Finally, prepare the files for the printers.

Don't forget the response mechanisms and calls to action:

- Do tell them to buy/visit the website
- Include your URL
- Include your phone number
- Include your social media locations

Top Tip
Direct Mail Pointers

Here are a few things it's worth knowing about direct mail and catalogues before you start:

- Printing costs are ruled by the 4 times table. The better the number of pages in the catalogue fits into the 4 times table, the cheaper it will be to print (per page). If you can divide it by 16, it's going to be better than if you can only divide it by 8. Therefore a 64-page book is much cheaper per page than a 56-page one.
- Print your cover separately, using heavier paper than used for the contents. So your 32-page book becomes a 32-page book with a 4-page cover.
- With a heavy cover, you can get away with a much lighter inner paper – the heavier the paper you use, the more clay is in it, and the more expensive it is to buy and post.
- Whether you're doing a catalogue or a postcard, the size of the mailing piece may well impact on the price of postage, printing, paper, binding and mailing – so check this!
- Consider going naked. If you mail your catalogue without any polywrap, it will save you money and you can get some environmental discounts too. Some companies have also reported that it increases response.
- You can rent space in your mailings. If you are sending out a mailing in an envelope or polywrap, you can allow other businesses to insert a leaflet and they'll pay you for the privilege. List brokers are a good place to start if you are interested in doing this. They'll also help you find people who will pay to be included in your product parcels.

Paper, print, bind

In order to turn your designs into reality, you need to source the paper, organise the printers and, if you have multiple pages, get the whole thing bound together. Your printers may be able to do all three stages, but often you will need to use a separate binding house – so make sure you have got the number of a good courier in case you need them.

You will also be given the opportunity to proof your mailing on press. If you have high production values, then this is a really important step to commit to. This is your opportunity to make sure the mailing looks just right.

Back when I looked after mailing campaigns for Past Times, we produced a Christmas-themed, self-sealed mailing piece that went out to about 100,000 people. It was a really clever piece, personalised with the map and address of the local store and it did drive a great response: a response that would probably have been better if one of us had gone to proof it on press and realised that the colour mix on the red was wrong. As it was, we posted 100,000 **pink** Christmas mailings. Make sure you don't make that mistake!

Posting and mailing

Once your mailing piece is ready, you need to get it into the post.

Over the last few years, this has become very complex: it's not just Royal Mail (which was complex enough); there are now lots of different routes into the postal system.

The biggest determinant of how much you pay in postage is the size and weight of the mailing piece. Once that is set, though, there is more you can do to further reduce the costs.

- If you are not in a hurry for your mailing to land, you can send it even slower than second class, usually landing within seven days.
- If you can get your mailing data right, you can also prepare it for the postal service by putting it in the right order – that's called MailSort or WalkSort. This means it is easier for the Royal Mail to process, so again you'll pay less.

In addition to the postage, you'll also need a mailing house to address and mail it (and polywrap it, if you need that done). It's worth talking to a mailing house, or postage specialist, early in the process to make sure you get the right deal and service.

Shops and shows

Having a shop or running a stand at shows can be a great way to recruit new customers. The number one aim of either is to sell product there and then, but you should also be aiming to gather customer details (to mail them and email them) and make them aware of your website.

You should have your website address clearly on anything they leave with – bag, receipt, flyer, etc. The website address should also be clearly visible to anyone in the shop/stand or walking past; put it on the shop windows and any other big wall spaces you have.

Less than 10% of people who come into your shop or stall will buy – so try and at least get the data of the others. Having a sign-up competition to gather details is very effective – just a postcard-sized form for people to fill in with a prize of gift vouchers can generate a lot of extra data.

Advertising

Our focus is on the forms of advertising that can drive a direct response:

- Off-the-page advertising
- Inserts

Both these focus on print journalism, which is great because it means you can easily target the right type of people. When you run a customer survey, ask them which magazines and newspapers they read and that will give you your list of titles to advertise in.

Both these methods have been used for decades by the mail-order industry to recruit new customers and they are still working today.

Off-the-page adverts are the ones you see in the back of every section of every weekend paper, usually focused on an offer for one particular product, with an order form at the bottom of the page. If you are going down this route, engage a design agency that specialises in this type of advert; getting a great response is a science.

Done well, off-the-page advertising can provide you with a customer recruitment vehicle that makes a profit!

If you want to get serious with off-the-page, have your adverts ready and call the papers on a Friday to see what last-minute space they have. You can usually snap that up at a huge discount. No one ever pays Rate-Card prices, so always ask for a discount.

If you are producing a catalogue or a flyer, you should test **inserting** the catalogue in newspapers and magazines. It's much cheaper than cold mailing because you don't have the postage costs to worry about, but response rates tend to be lower. Find the right publication to insert into, though, and you'll find a great way to recruit new customers.

When Doesn't Offline Marketing Work?

As you have seen in this section, there are many forms of offline marketing. I struggle to think of any business that wouldn't benefit from mailing its existing customers – even if it's just a postcard to tell them the sale is on.

Offline marketing requires a different set of skills to online marketing and behaves very differently financially – you make the investment upfront and once the activity's gone out the door, there is nothing you can do to affect it.

Don't embark on offline marketing until your business is ready: the systems can cope with it, you've got the cash and you have access to the expertise to make it work.

....

What to Measure in Offline Marketing

Activity	Distribution	Cost	Cost per Item	Orders	Value	AOV	Response Rate	Cost/Profit per Order
Mailing to List A	5,000	7,000	1.4	51	3,570	70	1%	-67.25
Mailing to List B	5,000	5,000	1	102	6,120	60	2%	1.17
Insert in Magazine A	5,000	3,000	0.6	25	1,250	50	0.5%	-70

Below are the key metrics you need to be measuring; most are in the table above:

- Distributed
- Cost
- Cost per Item
- Orders
- Value
- AOV
- Response Rate
- Cost/Profit per order

For more information on each of these metrics, see Chapter 10.

It is likely that most of the marketing activity you do offline (exclude mailing your housefile) will be unprofitable. So you also need to track how the customers you recruit via each method go on to behave over the coming months: do they keep ordering from you?

(This then builds up to the concept of Customer Lifetime Value – that's discussed in the first book in this series *eCommerce MasterPlan 1.8*. You can get hold of it at **eCommerceMasterPlan.com/Books**)

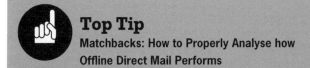

Top Tip
Matchbacks: How to Properly Analyse how Offline Direct Mail Performs

Back in *eCommerce MasterPlan 1.8*, I wrote about the attribution debate in online marketing. Well, the matchback process I'm going to outline here is a way to make sure all the sales from your direct marketing activity are attributed back to the source of the data. This isn't full attribution, as it only looks at one marketing method.

The matchback process is a fairly simple one, but is the only way to understand how well each of your cold data lists has performed. Matchbacks solve these two issues:

- When you prepare data for a mailing, you have to de-dupe it to ensure that each person only gets one copy of the mailing. That de-dupe process is necessary because when you are buying and swapping cold lists, you will get names of people that are already on your own database and some people will appear on more than one of the lists you buy. De-duping makes sure you only mail the right people, but it also means that you are not getting a full picture of how well each list really works for you.
- It is increasingly difficult to track the sales response from Direct Mail because that requires getting the customers to enter a code on the website, or tell you that code when they call up.

To prepare for a matchback, you need to pull together:

- Each of your original (pre de-dupe) cold mailing files.
- Which lists were sent to whom for each mailing.
- Mailing dates.
- How long each mailing was valid for – the period after it mailed in which you believe it will have generated a response (this is usually between four and eight weeks).
- A full list of orders placed during the season – name, address, and value.

Then simply reallocate any order that came in from someone on each list during the period that mailing was valid.

This will give you the true value of each data source. The total will be higher than your sales total for the season because you are double-counting – but you will get the right metrics to be able to truly compare list performance and decide on activity for next time.

Successful Offline Marketing Checklist

- Can you use offline marketing to encourage repeat purchases? Recruit new customers?
- Prepare for a long testing process.
- Test more than one method.
- Make sure you have the necessary funds.
- Tap into the knowledge of those who have done it before.

WEBSITE

Visit **eCommerceMasterPlan.com** for more information on offline marketing.

NOTES

What are the key points from this section?

_____

_____

_____

_____

_____

_____

_____

_____

Other Notes:

_____

_____

_____

_____

_____

_____

_____

_____

_____

CHAPTER 6

Search Marketing

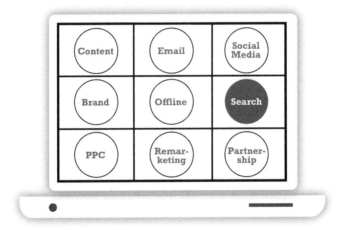

Search Marketing is "free" traffic from search engines.

By "free", I mean that you haven't directly paid for that traffic (like you would with a Google AdWords PPC account). Of course, search marketing isn't free: you may have paid an agency or your website builders and there's all the time you have spent working on optimising the content and creating it, too.

It's a complex art that's becoming both simpler and harder as time passes and the search algorithms change; simpler because there are ever-fewer methods to employ, harder because the quick wins are disappearing. This section has huge overlaps with both Content and Social Media – both those chapters could have been subsections of this one!

GRADUATES

This method is particularly useful for these **eCommerce Business Structures**:

- Online Only
- Mail Order
- Big Bricks and Clicks
- Boutique Bricks and Clicks
- Full Multichannel

Product Range Scale – so much easier if niche!
It is also going to be really powerful for you if your **USP** is:

- Knowledge and Information – because at the core of any successful search marketing strategy is great content

Why Should You Use Search Marketing if You Are an eCommerce Business?

Search marketing is a source of free traffic to your website. If you can increase traffic, and make sure it's traffic worth having (traffic that converts to sales), then it can be one of the most effective ways to grow your eCommerce business. It's powerful because:

- If you build your traffic in the right way, you will create a dependable source of traffic, sales and customers that you don't need to spend much money to attract.

This can be so powerful that for some businesses it becomes their way to beat the competition.

....

Search Marketing Objectives for eCommerce Businesses

It will take months for your Search Marketing activity to pay off; possibly more than a year. So you need to be committed to it for the long haul.

The ultimate objectives (whether that happens within 3 months, 6 months, or 2 years) need to be driving sales and attracting new customers, as well as making sure existing customers can find you when they should be buying from you.

It takes a while for your search marketing effort to pay off; to make sure it does, you need to pay close attention to the story that sits under the sales and ROI – so look at the traffic volumes, the sources of that traffic, how many and via which keywords that traffic comes, and also how the traffic behaves on your website.

How Search Marketing Works

The search marketing we are discussing here is broader than just traditional SEO (Search Engine Optimisation). That was focused on getting you to position number one by optimising your website and getting inbound links. Search marketing is now far more complex than that because:

- **Universal Search** means that there are now multiple ways to get into the search engine results pages (SERPs) – map, social media, image, video and more.
- **Increasingly Sophisticated Algorithms** mean that trying to manipulate the "normal" search results (the preserve of SEO) is becoming ever harder – the quick wins are disappearing.
- **Some links are bad** – in 2012, for the first time, Google penalised sites based on links from "bad" websites – so you don't want to risk getting the wrong links!
- Caring about **position one is a distraction**. We care about traffic – position one for ego terms is a waste of all our efforts.
- It's **not just about links** anymore – it's also social media; you need to be talked about.
- **Personalised Search** is here. Google gives you different results based on where you are in the world (just search for "takeaway"); if you are logged in to Google, it will also give you results based on websites you have been to before; and if you have a Google+ account, the results you see will be influenced by what the people you are connected to have looked at and Liked. This is just the tip of the personalised search iceberg.

Top Tip
Why Google?

Most search marketers focus on Google because it is the biggest: it has over 80% of the search market in the UK and in the USA. Doing well on Google will bring the most traffic and therefore the most sales.

Google is also the most sophisticated search engine; it's writing the rule book. Anything you do to be better on Google will probably be the same thing you need to do to be better on the other search engines.

If you are looking at international sales, make sure you are focused on the right search engine for that marketplace. In China, the biggest is www.baidu.com, with about 75% of the market share; in Russia, it's www.yandex.com with about 60% of the market share.

How do we manage the changes? What do we need to do?

First we need to stop worrying about Google. Stop obsessing about the latest algorithm change and getting worried about position one and start building a site that deserves to receive traffic. It is possible to spend many hours and days trying to work out what the latest algorithm changes mean and how to "do SEO" in order to keep your traffic volumes up; but that's time that could be better spent elsewhere. I prefer to keep in mind what Google is actually trying to do.

Larry Page (co-founder and CEO of Google) described the "perfect search engine" as something that "… understands exactly what you mean and gives you back exactly what you want".

This remains Google's objective and is why the fundamentals of how to get search traffic have never changed. Search success continues to come down to achieving three things:

- be **in** the search engine's index
- be **relevant** to the users' search
- be **important** enough to appear on the SERPs

"Be in" means they know you exist – that means they have your site listed in their index and listed accurately.

WEBSITE
see **eCommerceMasterPlan.com/Free** for a guide to checking this.

"Be relevant" means your site/content/pages contain the right keywords.

"Be important" means for all the relevant sites in the index there are more "this is great" signals for your site than any other.

We need to make sure our website is the best possible result for the keywords we care about, the site that *should* be returned for a search.

Practically, this means:

- Take advantage of every route into the search engine's index you can (be **in**)
- Optimise your website with the right keywords (be **relevant**)
- Create great content that customers will appreciate (be **relevant/ important**)
- Prove you're the best through social chatter and links (be **important**)

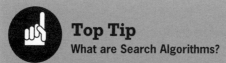

Top Tip
What are Search Algorithms?

A search engine's algorithm is a very complex piece of software that analyses millions of pieces of data to return the search results. Each search engine has its own algorithm and each one assesses the contents of its index and delivers results differently. When you hear about an algorithm change, it means that the search engine has changed the way in which it assesses the data, for example:

● Something that previously made a site important, doesn't any more (or vice versa)

● They have started taking something into account that they didn't before (or vice versa)

● Or hundreds of other options

It's very hard to anticipate what the next change will be and (of course) no search engine tells us exactly what its algorithm does, when it is changed, or if it is changed. This is why it's important to focus on what the search engine is trying to achieve rather than obsess about the individual changes.

Take advantage of every route into the search results

The routes in change, so keep an eye on what is appearing in the actual search results for your products and keywords. Then you can take advantage of new routes quickly.

The key "free" routes in are as follows.

Image search

Results: www.google.co.uk/imghp

This is Google's search engine of images. If you sell products that are particularly decorative, this can be really powerful.

Google automatically picks up images from your website, so you should optimise your images. This means getting all the text around them right – the alt text, the anchor text (if they link somewhere), the file name and the content on the page the image sits on.

You can also add image information to the Sitemap XML feed you provide via Webmaster Tools.

Google Maps

aka Google Place Pages

aka Google+ Place Pages

Tool: www.google.com/local/add/businessCenter

Results: maps.google.co.uk

These are the results that appear on Google Maps and also in the search results as locations.

If you have physical locations that people can visit, it's well worth getting your place page created and optimised.

The first thing to do is find out if you already have a place page. Google have created many automatically; if your business is already on Google Maps, you need to take control and confirm you are the business owner – a set of fairly simple steps.

If your business isn't already there, you need to go and get it set up. Once it exists, you can encourage people to review your business and also update it with any events or promotions you are running.

Video results

Tool: www.YouTube.com

Results: www.google.com/videohp

These are results that are videos.

You don't have to have your videos on YouTube to appear here, but it helps. YouTube is the second biggest search engine, so it makes sense to have your videos there anyway.

If you don't want your videos on YouTube, you need to provide a Video XML Feed to Google via Webmaster Tools.

Plus, make sure you have optimised your videos' names and description too.

News

Tool: support.google.com/news/publisher

Results: news.google.com

The news results are a Google manipulation of world news. When a story is a hot topic, the news results will show on the SERPs – often at the top.

If your site is a news source in its own right, you can submit it for inclusion in Google News. You can also create a news sitemap and submit that via Webmaster Tools.

If you only have an occasional story to submit, you can't do that directly. So get it onto a site that is included in Google News. Several of the PR newswires fit into this category.

WEBSITE
More details on the current options are on
eCommerceMasterPlan.com/Free

Top Tip
Webmaster Tools and Sitemaps

Each search engine has a "Webmaster Tools": a way for site owners to talk to the search engine about their site and what they are doing right or wrong. This extra data about how well your website is doing can enable you to get it fixed! It's also a way for website owners to raise their profile with the search engines by making sure that everything you want to be indexed actually is. That's done using XML Sitemaps; you should have one for your site's content and others for different types of content (Video, Images, News).

On Google, you can also integrate your Webmaster Tools with Google Analytics, which gives you some great data about your search performance. You can see the number of impressions you have had on each keyword and also which bits of your content are appearing the most often – really useful data.

Don't forget to create your sitemaps and submit them too. If you're not sure how to do this – speak to your site builder; it varies from site to site but shouldn't be difficult. To get set up, go to:

For Google: www.google.com/webmasters/tools
For Bing: www.bing.com/toolbox/webmaster

Create great content that customers will appreciate

As well as getting yourself into the Google index in as many ways as possible, what can you do to make sure you are going to get onto the SERPs enough to get the traffic you deserve? You have got to have the right content (see Chapter 1) – and it's got to be great content, content that works for you. It needs to be content people want to read and want to share; even better if it is content your target customers want to read and share. Content can just be a great product page.

As well as creating the content on your website, you need to make sure you have your social sharing buttons in place (see Chapter 3). Google is now seeing social shares as very important indicators of relevant websites – so you need to be doing everything you can to encourage your customers to share your content and talk about you on social media.

 **Top Tip**
DMOZ

DMOZ.org is the Open Directory Project. It is a project to try and humanly review all websites on the internet. It's important in search marketing because it's highly respected by Google and is where they launch their spiders from (the spiders research the internet to create Google's index). If you are not on Google's index, you won't get into the search results – so if the spiders don't find you, you won't be on Google. Luckily, DMOZ isn't the only way for Google to find your website, as it frequently takes months for someone to review your website; until you have been reviewed you can't be listed. As it only takes five minutes to request listing – make sure you do it for your website.

Optimise your website with the right keywords

WORKBOOK
Download our Search Keywords Workbook from the website at **eCommerceMasterPlan.com/Free**

So far we have discussed how to get into the search engine index and how to make Google think you are important enough to be seen on the first page (content and social media), but we've not looked at how to make sure you appear for the correct things – be **relevant**.

Being relevant is critical – if you appear for the right things you'll get more traffic and that traffic will be of a better quality – more likely to buy. Becoming relevant means identifying the right keywords for your site and then putting them in place. Getting this right can be really powerful. I've seen this have a massive impact on traffic and more importantly, creating conversions – sometimes even doubling them!

It has a big and quick impact because it makes a difference to how Google sees your website almost overnight.

Identify the right keywords

First brainstorm what the keywords for your website might be. Don't just do this yourself – ask the rest of the business. Gather them in an Excel spreadsheet. Then add keywords that have brought you traffic in the past (you should be able to get this from Google Analytics); add these to the spreadsheet. If you have PPC on the go (or ever have), get the keywords from that as well and add them to the spreadsheet.

At this point you may also want to consult a few keyword tools (the Google one is pretty good and free) to let them suggest keywords you have missed. Add these to the spreadsheet.

Once you have your very large spreadsheet (several thousand is great), you need to gather some data on those keywords so you can see which are good and which are bad. So add the following data in, if possible, for each keyword:

- Search volumes – you can get them free from Google Keyword Tool.
- Previous search traffic performance – what the keywords have previously done for you. At a minimum, you want clicks, conversion rate, and bounce rate. Get them from Google Analytics.
- PPC Data – again, to see what the keywords have previously done for you. At a minimum you want visits and conversion rate.
- Position Report – where your website is right now on the search engines, a ranking report.

It will take a while to gather the data and even longer to analyse it, but it's worth it. Once you have considered all the data, you should be able to see:

- Which keywords offer the biggest opportunity – those with large traffic volumes
- Which keywords work for you – those that have converted in the past and have low bounce rates
- Which keywords you are going to win on the fastest – those you are already ranking well for, or already getting traffic from

Now you have found the best keywords to aim for, you need to get them onto your website.

Getting the keywords onto your website

The first step is to tie the keywords to pages: which page would be the best for each keyword to be on? You only really want one or two keywords per page. You want a page that is about the keyword (you don't want to put "curtains" on a page about wall paint) and the more important the keyword, the closer to your site's main landing page it should be – so either the homepage or a category page. You might find that the results of the keyword analysis lead you to want to change some of the site's structure and create new pages where the search opportunities are.

Once that is done, you'll probably have between 5 and 20 pages where you really want to optimise the keywords. The rest of the site can have its keywords optimised automatically; that's one of the great things you can do with an eCommerce website.

Optimising the keywords means putting them into the right places:

- Title tag – the most important place for your keywords (consumers don't really see this; see "eCommerce MasterPlan - Your 5 Step..." below).

- Meta Description tag – not critical, but you do need it to be different on every page, so it is worth doing at the same time (consumers don't see this).
- H tags – these should be the headings in the copy on the page and are usually your category and product names. Each page needs one H1 tag, and then more H2s and H3s as necessary.
- You also want to get the alt text right on the images.

Source code of eCommerceMasterPlan.com showing title and description tags

For your chosen pages, you will need to write the Title tag and Meta Description tag. The Title tag should be relatively short and focused (under 75 characters) and have the keywords at the beginning (apart from the homepage, where the first words should be your brand name). The Meta Description needs to be about the page, for example:

Title tag: Ladies Red Shoes from the shoe shop

Meta Description: At the shoe shop we stock a wide range of ladies shoes in red, including boots, slingbacks, court shoes and sandals. Order today for free delivery in the UK.

Alt text is the alternative text for each image and should describe what's on the image.

Once they are all written, you need to put them in place on the website. You might be able to do this via your CMS, (Content Management System) but if not, your website builder will be able to do it for you.

Then you need to get the **automatic tags** done. For this you will almost certainly need to brief your website builder, covering the following:

- The automatic tagging on the pages should also work for new pages that are created. This should be a one-off exercise.
- If a tag is supplied manually, that should overwrite the automatic tagging.
- Alt text on all product images should be set as: "{product name} from the shoe shop".
- Title tag on all product pages should be set as "{product name} – {category name} from the shoe shop".
- Title tag on all category pages should be set as "{category name} from the shoe shop".
- Title tag on all other pages should be set as "{page name} from the shoe shop".
- Meta Description on all product pages should be set as "At the shoe shop we stock a wide range of {product name}, including boots, slingbacks, court shoes and sandals. Order today for free delivery in the UK".
- Meta Description on all category pages should be set as "At the shoe shop we stock a wide range of {product name}, including boots, slingbacks, court shoes and sandals. Order today for free delivery in the UK".
- Meta Description on all other pages should be set as "{page name}. At the shoe shop we stock a wide range of {product name}, including boots, slingbacks, court shoes and sandals. Order today for free delivery in the UK".
- OR Meta Description should lift the first X characters of product/ category copy.

As soon as Google picks up on all of that being in place (usually within a week), you should see an impact on search traffic volume to your website, a greater number of keywords driving that traffic and the quality of the traffic improving.

Don't think you can forget about your keywords. You will need to review whether or not you chose the right ones. Did they bring in conversions? If not, you may need to amend them in 6 or 12 months' time. You also need to keep remembering what your most important keywords are and include them as you create and optimise your content.

· ·

When Doesn't Search Marketing Work?

If you have a site built in Flash, it's going to be very hard to optimise it to get you search traffic.

Other than that, every business selling online should be aware of how to get traffic from the search engines.

Even if you are PiggyBacking (using someone else's website), getting the keywords for your products right will bring you more sales, both from search results on the PiggyBack site (think of it as its own little search engine) and from helping the piggyback site appear in the SERPs.

What to Measure in Search Marketing

Traffic Sources	Visits	Bounce Rate	Cost	Orders	Value	AOV	Conversion Rate	Sales/ Visit
Google	5,000	30%	2,000	26	1,820	70	5%	36.4p
Bing	5,000	35%	500	35	1,575	45	8%	31.5p

Below are the key metrics you need to be measuring for your search marketing; most are in the table above. The performance of your search marketing will improve over time, so compare the trends over time:

- Visits
- Bounce rate
- Orders
- Conversion rate
- Sales
- AOV
- Sales per visit
- No of X driving traffic
- Impressions
- Click-through rate

For more information on each of these metrics, see Chapter 10.

I haven't included positions here because search is about the quality of the traffic and how well it converts, not about whether or not you are in first position. Saying that, improving your rankings will increase traffic, so there's no harm in checking them every 3 to 6 months, just don't get distracted by them.

Successful Search Marketing Checklist

- Be In – Have you covered all the routes into the search results that you can?
- Be Relevant – Is the website fully optimised? Keywords and tags?
- Be Relevant – Are you creating content?
- Be Important – Have you incorporated search objectives into your social media activity?
- Check you're still using the right keywords

WEBSITE

Visit **eCommerceMasterPlan.com** for the latest information on search marketing, what's new, what Google has done now, and how it all relates to eCommerce businesses.

NOTES

What are the key points from this section?

_____

_____

_____

_____

_____

_____

_____

_____

_____

Other Notes:

_____

_____

_____

_____

_____

_____

_____

_____

_____

CHAPTER 7

PPC (Pay Per Click) Marketing

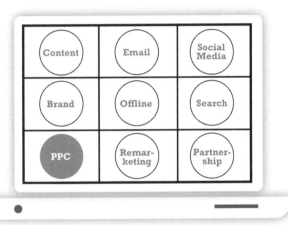

PPC, like the previous chapter topic, is about getting traffic from search engines – getting the traffic that brings you sales. The difference is that, because you're paying, there's no waiting to get this traffic – you select a keyword and how much you want to pay and then you have traffic. PPC means Pay Per Click. It can be used to refer to any advertising where you pay for each click to your website. For the purposes of this chapter, we are focusing on search PPC (using either Google AdWords or Microsoft adCenter), but we will also discuss using it on Facebook and LinkedIn.

GRADUATES

This method works for all, but it is particularly essential for this **eCommerce Business Structure**:

- Online Only

It works for any **Product Range Scale**.
It is also particularly useful if your **USP** is:

- Products
- Price
- And will work more effectively if your brand is strong

Why Should You Use PPC?

PPC marketing can be a really effective way to quickly build a stream of quality traffic to your website. But it will only work well if your products are right for PPC, if there isn't too much competition and if your offering is good. The strengths of PPC are:

- You get traffic really fast – you don't need to wait as with SEO, or until you have a big enough email database. As long as you can afford the clicks, you can get traffic to your site within minutes.
- You are in total control – you select where your ads will be shown, you set how much you are willing to pay and you can stop it at any time with immediate effect.
- It is very flexible – changing things is very easy and the changes happen almost immediately, so you can react to changing situations fast, such as products going out of stock.

PPC Marketing Objectives for eCommerce Businesses

PPC activity will mainly be focused on recruiting new customers and on driving sales. It can be expensive, so you don't want to be relying on it to get your existing customers back to you.

The number one thing to watch is your sales vs. your cost – are they within your ROI targets?

Top Tip
PPC Glossary

- Adtext = an advert that is just text
- Click = when someone sees your ad and clicks on it – taking them through to your website (this is what you pay for)
- CPC = cost per click = the amount you've paid for each click
- CTR = click-through rate = the rate at which those who have seen your ad have clicked on it
- Impression = number of times your ads are seen
- Placement = a website on which your ad appears
- Quality score (QS) = how good your keyword/ad/landing page is
- Bid = how much you are willing to pay for a click
- Conversion = an order placed as a result of PPC
- View-Through Conversion = an order placed by someone who's seen your ad on the content network but hasn't clicked on it
- Search Network = the search pages that the search engine puts your keyword-triggered adverts on
- Content Network = the non-search pages (placements) that the search engine puts your adverts on – these are usually on blogs and news websites

How PPC Marketing Works

You set up an account with one of the PPC services (Google etc.), create ads and tell the system how you want those ads targeted (at people searching on a keyword, searching for certain products, or those interested in certain things). The ads are then shown and each time someone clicks on the ad (on a link to a page on your website) you are charged the agreed fee.

PPC accounts are VERY easy to set up (under 30 minutes, usually), but take a lot of work to get right. Anyone can use them to generate traffic to their website; as an eCommerce business, you don't want any old traffic; you want quality traffic – traffic that's going to buy from you. You also need traffic that does not cost too much. The performance needs to fit with your ROI (profit) objectives.

The good news is you can optimise your PPC account to make sure the traffic you get is quality traffic and thus keep it within your ROI objectives. We are going to look at how to optimise PPC, but before you do anything, you need to understand the key number in Pay Per Click.

WORKBOOK
To make the most of this chapter, go to
eCommerceMasterPlan.com/Free and download the
accompanying workbook.

Your cost/sales, or "cost as a percentage of sales"

Those of you who have read *eCommerce MasterPlan* will remember this from Chapter 5, *Building Your Business for Profit and Growth*. (If you'd like to get yourself a copy, it's available at **eCommerceMasterPlan. com/Books**)

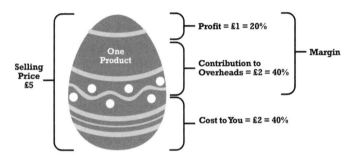

We know that the value of each sale the website generates is split three ways to cover:

- the cost of the products bought
- a contribution to company overheads
- profit (what is left)

Part of this profit piece is what you'll be spending on click costs. In this case the target cost/sales would be 20% (1 divided by 5). That would give you a break even cost of recruitment, if you want to make a profit make it lower than 20%, or if you know you can afford to lose money on the first order make it higher than 20%.

This is a really useful number to have because it makes it REALLY EASY to see how well your PPC activity is doing. Almost every PPC

performance report you'll ever look at has the cost and the sales figure –
giving you all the numbers you need to see if you are on target or not.

You can use cost as a percentage of sales to compare keywords, ads,
adgroups – anything in Pay Per Click. Please work this figure out before
you do ANYTHING else in PPC.

Most businesses will need to run at cost/sales of 20% or higher to get
enough traffic for the activity to be worthwhile.

PPC structure and strategy

Something you want to get right when you start with PPC is to get your
account set up correctly. (The following is based on Google AdWords'
structure, but Microsoft adCenter/Bing Ads works in a very similar way.)

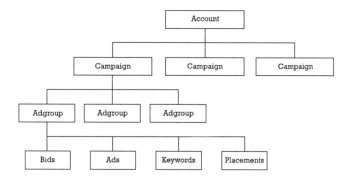

Before you start building your account, work out how you're going to
structure it. Think about:

- **Reporting** It is really easy to produce reports at Campaign Level and Adgroup Level. So you should structure these to be areas you might want to look at and compare.

- **Optimisation and Quality Score** The game with PPC is to get the best traffic possible for the lowest possible cost. This means taking everything to the nth degree and really focusing on the niches. (The nth degree would be each keyword having its own adgroup – we don't want to set all that up on day one because we don't know if it will be worth it.) We need each adgroup to be full of very similar keywords that can all use the same ads and link to the same landing page. This makes the account much easier to use and to optimise and also increases our quality score (which brings costs down).

- **Budgets and other Campaign-Level Only Settings** There are certain critical settings that can only be set at the campaign level. These change from time to time – so double-check them before making the decision – but broadly include budgets (how much you'll pay per month/day), devices (mobile? desktop?), content network, and geographic areas.

So how should you structure your account? For an eCommerce business, this should be relatively straightforward because the structure of your PPC account will most likely follow the structure of your website navigation – so long as that's well structured! Here are some examples.

Example: fashion retailer's campaigns

We've split the campaigns this way to see at a glance how the different genders are performing and work out how to allocate the budget between them.

Example: fashion retailer's adgroups within the women's wear campaign

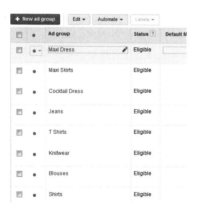

The adgroups are split out by product type; which means the keywords are easily focused. We have several adgroups for skirts because the types of skirt are very different. The blouse and shirt adgroups will both go to the same landing page because some women call them 'shirts' and some 'blouses' and they will perform better if the adtext matches the keywords.

Now we have the structure for Women's wear, we'll follow the same theory to roll out to Children and Men's.

Example: furniture retailer

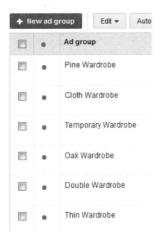

Top Tip
Quality Score

The Quality Score (QS) is used by Microsoft and Google to assess the quality of your adverts. It is a score out of 10, given at keyword level; 10 is best and to get 10 your keyword, ad and landing page need to be in harmony. For example: if your keyword is "blue mugs", your adtext should be about blue mugs and your landing page should be all about blue mugs.

But if your keyword is "cool mugs" and your adtext is about blue mugs and your landing page has mugs of all colours, you are going to get a much poorer quality score.

- On Google, it helps to determine where your ads appear, so a good QS means you will get a high position (and more traffic) for less money.
- On Microsoft it is less critical, but does indicate how likely your ads are to appear.

Improving your Quality Score is really important if you want to get the most traffic and best-quality traffic with your click budget. All the optimisation tactics we are discussing in this chapter support improving your QS.

Brand bidding

One of the oldest questions in PPC is: should you bid on your own name? The short answer is yes, because:

- As we saw in Chapter 6, the SERPs are constantly changing, so we need to create as many ways as possible to be there and PPC is one.
- Being in first position **and** having the paid ad gives you much more of the screen, thus increasing the chances of being clicked on.
- Some people click paid ads, some click non-paid.
- It's really not very expensive – you should be paying a lot less than 10p per click and the ROI should be huge. So it's a fairly cheap insurance policy to make sure your customers find your website.

But if you are going to bid on your brand terms, do it in a separate campaign and report on it separately. A brand campaign will often have a cost/sales of just 1–5% – that's a phenomenally good performance. You don't want that making your overall results look better than they are.

The keywords in your brand adgroup should include your brand name, your website address and common misspellings: both phonetic and typos. For indiumonline (my marketing agency), we bid on keywords such as: indium, indyum, iridium, indian, chloe thomas, indiumonline.co.uk, etc.

Top Tip
Keyword Match Types

Keyword match types are a fundamental part of optimising your PPC account and there are four keyword match types:

Match Type	Example: What it looks like in your account	How it works	Where in the account?
Broad	Red dress	Your ads will appear for any search where Google or Microsoft feel it will be relevant. That might include: • crimson dress • dresses in dark pink • blue dress	Set up in adgroups
Phrase	"red dress"	Your ads will only appear when someone searches on the phrase on its own, or with text before or after the phrase: • red dress • buy a red dress • red dress for Ascot	Set up in adgroups
Exact	[red dress]	Your ads will only display when someone searches on red dress – they won't appear for anything else	Set up in adgroups
Negative	-blue	Your ads won't appear for phrases with this keyword in. Frequently used negatives are "second hand", "how to", etc.	Either at campaign or adgroup level

Start at broad. If a keyword performs well as one, test it as the other match types, because you'll get a different response from each.

How to optimise

To make your PPC successful, you must optimise – continuously.

From the day you first launch your PPC activity, it will always need optimising. The optimisation process never ends and is particularly intense for the first few months after you make major changes.

Please do not turn it on and leave it!!

We have already identified our performance target – the cost/sales percentage. The job of optimisation is to hit that, to:

- Identify the activity that is failing to meet the target and penalise it (turn it off, or optimise it down)
- Identify the activity that is performing ahead of that target and promote it (spend more here, roll it out)

There are lots of levels and areas to look at while optimising: campaign, adgroup, keyword, placement and more, so it's important to fully understand what is happening before optimising badly. For example:

- Our Target Cost/Sales = 30%
- Our Women's Campaign is performing at 40%

Should we turn it off?

Let's look deeper:

- Within the Women's Campaign, all adgroups are within the target, apart from "Jeans", which is at 60%.

Should we turn it off?

No, let's look deeper:

- Within the Jeans adgroup, we have 10 keywords; 5 of those are performing within the target, 4 have yet to drive a sale and the keyword "Jeans" is performing at 70%.

By looking deeper, we have identified that the only issue is the keyword "Jeans", so we need to optimise just that keyword down, but leave everything else.

Optimising up and down

I've been going on about "optimising" all chapter – but not yet explained how to do it. Well, optimising PPC is one area where no matter how many hours and years you spend doing it, you're always learning – and I can't fit all that in one book! What I can provide you with, though, is this handy guide to the most common forms of optimisation – understand these and you're far ahead of most PPC account owners.

Level	Optimise Up	Optimise Down
Keyword	Increase bid Add more keyword match types	Decrease bid Change match type to a more strict one Pause
Adtext	Create another copy Pause other ads	Turn off Test a different version Try linking to a different page
Placements	Turn into a managed placement Increase the bid	Decrease the bid Turn it into a negative placement (so your ads don't appear there)
Adgroups	Increase default bid Split out into more niche adgroups	Decrease default bid Pause
Campaigns	Increase budget Widen targeting	Decrease budget Pause

These are the key ways to optimise your account. There are others and they change over time as Microsoft and Google create new tools, but these are your key methods. Take the time to master them.

We also need to understand how much we need to spend on each keyword before we can tell if it works or not. This is your AOV (or product price) multiplied by your cost/sales percentage. For example:

Cost/Sales Percentage = 30%
AOV = £50

$$\left[£50 \times 30\% = £15 \right]$$

The amount you need to
spend before you can
validly give up on a keyword = £15

If the AOV was £100:

$$\left[£100 \times 30\% = £30 \right]$$

You need to understand this number so you know when to turn off a keyword. In the example, if you start turning off keywords that have only had £5 spent on them, you are a long way from knowing if that keyword would work for you or not.

Ads and landing pages

The layout of an eCommerce site restricts how much you can change your landing pages. After all, if you are bidding on "Trousers", you want to link to the trousers category – there's not much choice beyond that. But where you do have options, it's always good to test them; see which traffic converts best on each page.

Pine Wardrobe
furniture.co.uk/PineWardrobes
Big Selection of Pine Wardrobes
All available next day delivery

Where you have a lot of scope for testing is the ads and there is so much you can test within the ads, so much that you should be testing. Generally, I recommend people to get the keyword optimisation right before starting on the adtext testing; once you're ready for testing the ads, the first things you should be testing are:

Element	What to test	Lessons to roll out
Headline	Including your brand name or not The text itself Capitalisation	Brand name or not Capitalisation
Body text	Including your brand name or not The text itself Capitalisation Including the price Including delivery price	Including your brand name or not Capitalisation Including the price Including delivery price
Display URL	Including www. or not Capitalisation Domain vs. something afterwards, e.g. yourdomain.com or yourdomain.com/widget	Including www. or not Capitalisation Domain vs. something afterwards, e.g. yourdomain.com or yourdomain.com/widget

Only ever test one of these at a time within each adgroup. When you learn something that it is possible to roll out, do, but check that performance really does improve across the account; don't just assume it will.

Other ways to get PPC traffic

Most of what we've discussed in this chapter has been exclusively about using keywords to advertise within the search engine results of Google (via Google AdWords), Yahoo, or Bing (both via Microsoft adCenter). Here are some other options it may be worth testing.

Placements and the Content Network

There is another set of ads open to you if you are using either Microsoft or Google, which you should be testing and optimising. These put your adverts onto websites (placements) via the Content Network/Display Network. Within this are site owners who have "sold" part of their pages to Google via the Google AdSense program.

Google chooses where to show your adverts based on how well the keywords in your adgroup match the content of the web page. So if your adgroup is about curtains, your ads will start to get placements on websites about interior design and curtains. This should be a good thing, but you need to keep an eye on their performance, optimising individual placements up and down depending on their performance.

Product Listing Ads (PLAs)

This is the newest option available on Google AdWords (not available on Microsoft's Bing Ads at the time of writing). PLAs aren't just a new form of Ad, they're also a new way to target – they're not based on either keywords or placements. Both targeting and the ads are created from the products themselves.

To run PLAs, you need to provide a feed of all your products (well, all those you want to advertise) to Google via the Google Merchant Center, and link that to your AdWords account.

From the feed, you can create groups of products to advertise – your mugs, your dresses, the Parker pens, etc.

WEBSITE
Find out more about PLAs and what they're doing to eCommerce businesses on the website **eCommerceMasterPlan.com**

Quick tips for you:

- Do test it – it's bringing some great ROI results for eCommerce businesses – so please test it.
- Have more than one adgroup – I've seen a few accounts with all their products in one adgroup; that's really untargeted and isn't going to bring you great results.
- Think about what you want to do before you set up a feed; most of the optimisation power comes from what you put into the feed in the first place. So get it right.

On Facebook and LinkedIn

In addition to PPC advertising on the search engines, you can now also do it on Facebook and LinkedIn. These operate in a very similar way to the search engines, but with one key difference: you are targeting people based on who they are rather than what they are searching for.

This can be very cool: for example, if you sell wedding favours, you can target people whose Facebook relationship status is "Engaged"; if you sell equestrian clothing, you can target people interested in horses. If you sell stair lifts, you can target those aged over 70. But it is much harder to make these ads work within your ROI targets than with normal PPC.

Stay in control of your testing

The danger with PPC is that there's so much to test you just go test crazy and have so many tests running that you can't work out what's causing any good or bad results.

To control this, keep a record of what you are testing (as simple as a Word document or actual notepad) and remember to check it. When you want to, run another test so you can timetable your roll-outs. We saw above that it takes a while to optimise an account and that during that time you will spend a lot of click-cost testing. To avoid this, test and optimise some of your planned activity and only turn on more once you have that optimised. The more you spend, the faster you'll optimise, so limiting the number of tests will speed up your learning.

If you need to drive 1,000 clicks through an adgroup to optimise it, the total cost of those clicks is £500 (at 50p per click) and if your budget is only £200 per month, you are going to do much better if you spend months 1 and 2 getting one adgroup right. By month 3 you'll be driving sales pretty effectively. Then you can start the optimisation process again with adgroup 2. This also means you can factor in what you learnt with adgroup 1, so it should be quicker and cheaper to optimise adgroup 2.

The changing face of PPC

Microsoft and Google are constantly changing their PPC engines: what you can do, what you can't and all kinds of settings options. It's really important to keep on top of this, as fundamentally they are making the changes to make you keep spending more with them, not to improve your return – so not all the changes are going to suit you.

In this section we have run through the key fundamentals that remain the core of PPC success.

WEBSITE
On the website, **eCommerceMasterPlan.com** we have content examining the new things that come and go in PPC and how to make use of them. Please do check in every now and then, or sign up to the newsletter to make sure you are up to date.

. . . .

When Doesn't PPC Work?

I mentioned at the beginning that PPC doesn't work for every business. Why is that?

- In some sectors, the competition levels are so high that the price of a click means that you can't buy the traffic effectively.
- In other sectors, it's hard to find keywords that identify the searchers as your potential customers well enough.
- Other sectors are so price sensitive that you will get a lot of consumers price-comparing and not coming back to you to buy.

- Some products (like jewellery) are very style conscious – so it's hard to get the traffic that will convert just from keyword targeting.
- Some products have too low a price point – so if your AOV is under £10, you're really going to struggle.

What to Measure in PPC Marketing

Campaign	Impressions	Clicks	CTR%	Cost	Cost per Click	Orders	Value	AOV	Conversion Rate	Cost/ Sales
A	50,000	1,500	3%	555	37p	30	2,100	70	2%	26.4%
B	40,000	400	1%	180	45p	12	540	45	3%	33.3%

These are the key metrics you need to be measuring for your PPC marketing; most are in the table above:

- Impressions
- Clicks
- CTR %
- Cost
- Cost per Click
- Orders
- Sales
- AOV
- Conversion Rate
- Cost/Sales

For more information on each of these metrics, see Chapter 10.

You should use these tables to compare the performance of your PPC activity at any level; so from comparing Google AdWords and Microsoft adCenter to comparing individual keywords or adverts.

If you are running your PPC accounts well, you will be constantly optimising your activity, so it's really important to look at the results over lots of different time periods. I like to look at the last month and the last three months simultaneously, and also to compare what's happening now with what happened during the same period last year.

Successful PPC Marketing Checklist

- Know how much you can afford to spend to get each sale (your cost/ sales).
- Keep an eye on the settings and be ready for any changes to the software.
- Create and follow a launch and optimisation calendar.
- Keep an eye on what's happening in the business and make sure the PPC activity reflects this. Turn off products that aren't in stock; create ads for new products.
- Test, test, test.
- Regularly review the results.
- Optimise, optimise, optimise.

NOTES

What are the key points from this section?

_____

_____

_____

What is your cost/sales?

_____

_____

_____

How long can you run a keyword for?

_____

_____

_____

Other Notes:

_____

_____

_____

WEBSITE

Visit **eCommerceMasterPlan.com** for the latest information on PPC marketing, including what's changing and how to make the most of it.

CHAPTER 8 Remarketing

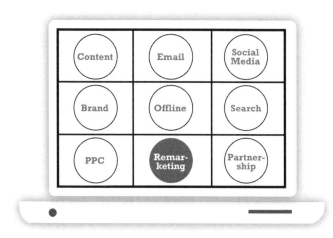

Remarketing is the newest marketing method in this book. It's all about advertising your business/website/products to people who've recently visited your website. Using your knowledge of what they look at on your site to advertise to them, if done right it should improve **all** your marketing.

GRADUATES

This method is particularly useful for these **eCommerce Business Structures**:

- Online Only
- Mail Order
- Big Bricks and Clicks
- Boutique Bricks and Clicks
- Full Multichannel

Along the **Product Range Scale** – it's easier to manage if you're a niche business, but works well for all.

It is not particularly useful for any individual **USP**, but if you are in a very competitive marketplace where customers shop around for the best offer or product, remarketing is a must: it will keep your website in the customers' thoughts.

Why Should You Use Remarketing if You Are an eCommerce Business?

Remarketing (also known as Retargeting) will make all your marketing activity more effective – so you'll have more sales and your marketing budget will go further. Essentially, it increases the ROI of all your marketing (both online and offline).

Does this sound too good to be true? It's not a magic bullet and takes some work to get it right, but used correctly it will bring great rewards. It is powerful because:

- You get the results very quickly – you are advertising to people who have already been to your site and seen the products, so they know what you are about and are already in the buying cycle.
- You are in total control – you are in control of the adverts and how much you are willing to pay for them. You also control who the ads are shown to, which pages of the site they had to view first and the demographics of those people. So you are in control of how efficiently the activity works and how strong the ROI becomes.
- You are targeting people you have already driven to your website once – so you are improving the performance of everything else you do to get people to your site.
- It should always be profitable – because you are in control of everything, it should always be possible to optimise it to be profitable.

Remarketing accounts I've worked on have seen substantially higher AOVs than normal PPC activity and frequently double-digit conversion rates too.

Remarketing Objectives for eCommerce Businesses

Remarketing activity should be focused on getting a good conversion rate and getting the right ROI. You have already paid to get these customers to your website once, so the remarketing activity MUST achieve your profit targets.

How Remarketing Works

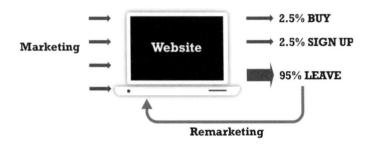

Remarketing

Remarketing enables you to advertise to people who have already been on your website in order to bring them back to buy from you again. This is done by dropping a cookie on the computer of people who visit certain pages of your site. Most eCommerce websites will convert at far less than 10%, meaning that at least 90% of visitors leave without giving you any information or buying. Remarketing targets those who leave, aiming to get them back again to buy.

So although throughout this chapter I'll be talking about targeting **people**, as with anything to do with cookies, you are actually targeting a certain machine. If I visit your website on my home laptop and have a remarketing cookie dropped on me, the remarketing ads will also appear when anyone else uses my home laptop; likewise, I won't see the remarketing ads when I use a different computer (unless I have been to your website on that computer too).

Key elements of remarketing

Software

The Remarketing Platform you use to serve the ads; without this you can't do Remarketing.

Website tagging

To enable remarketing, you need to put code on the pages of your site that will drop cookies on people in order to capture them so you can market to them later.

Cookie lengths aka Membership Duration

How long you keep visitors in your lists – how long they continue seeing your ads after they were last on your site (see Tip Box).

Ads

The ads get the customer back to your website; they can be text, image, or video.

Ad frequency

How many times per day does each person see your ads?

Segmentation

Which visitors see which ads, which pages of the site did they visit, etc.

Of these, the software is the only thing you can forget about once it's done; the other five need to be constantly monitored and considered within your optimisation process.

Choosing your remarketing platform

For many businesses, the choice of software is very limited: the only viable option is the Google AdWords platform. That's because it's cheap and easy to set up. The other providers either have a stated minimum traffic level or the fixed fees are so high you need a certain volume to make it worthwhile. It's always a good idea to test any online marketing before committing to it for the long haul – so the Google platform is the perfect place to do that.

Key reasons I think you should start with Google AdWords for Remarketing are:

- There is no set-up fee or subscription fee – you just pay for the clicks (similarly priced to "normal" Google PPC click costs).
- Google has a very large reach – so your ads can appear in lots of places.

- Anyone can use the Google Remarketing Platform – it's just part of the AdWords tool. There are no minimum spend and set-up costs, you can just do it.
- It's powerful: all the technology is there and the ads are shown on the Content Network – a vast collection of websites set up to display Google AdSense adverts. So your customers will be seeing your ads.

How to start remarketing

As with any new online marketing tool, it is really tempting to just go and get stuck in. But remarketing is a marketing method where sitting back for a bit and considering your plans can really benefit you and where there are a couple of things you have to do before anything is possible.

Step 1 – Amend your privacy policies

With remarketing, you're going to be capturing people's information in order to market to them – which means you need to make sure that this is covered in your privacy policy. You'll find a link to Google's instructions for the right approach in your country at **eCommerceMasterPlan. com/Free**

Step 2 – Implement the tag on your website

Tagging your site means putting some code on it to drop cookies. Until you have dropped cookies on people, you can't start any adverts (because you have got no one to show them to) and until you've put the tracking tags on your site, you won't be dropping any cookies.

The code is available from your Google AdWords account.

Even though you are going to start off showing the same ad to everyone, you don't necessarily want to capture everyone who visits your website. Pages for which you want to avoid capturing visitors and therefore don't want to put the tag onto, could be:

- Pages with high bounce rates – use Google Analytics to find them. You don't want people who are only looking at one page and leaving again. This probably includes your homepage.
- Pages designed for non-eCommerce customers. For example – PR pages, wholesale customer pages, supplier pages, staff logins. Some of these might not be visible from the main site – so think hard about them.

To avoid capturing them, you need to NOT put the tracking code on those pages. Once you've identified which pages you don't want to tag, create the brief for your web team and get the code in place.

While that's capturing your audience, you can move on to the next step.

Step 3 – Design your audience targeting

Audience is the name used for the groups of people you're going to be showing your ads to. The Number One rule is to start simply: one ad to everyone.

Although you are using a PPC platform to manage it all, you are targeting and testing people, not keywords. Starting simply enables you to identify some key benchmarks; running one ad will enable you to find out:

- Volume (how much your ads are going to show)
- Take up/response/scale – how well your visitors are going to respond to the ads – CTRs, conversion rates, AOVs, etc.

This shows you how much effort it will be worth putting into the optimisation, how much it's going to cost and the likely return.

Before anything goes live, you also need to design your future **Audience Targeting Strategy**.

Each audience can be defined by which pages they've visited. Before your ads can show, each audience you create needs to contain at least 100 people. In planning your targeting, you want to choose groups of pages that will enable that to happen – so for some low-traffic websites, you might only be able to use one audience. To check how quickly you are likely to get 100 people on any set of pages, look at the page views count in Google Analytics – how long does it take to get 100 visits? If it is over a month, it's probably not big enough to target.

There are pages on your site that are only looked at by certain types of customer, but for which we do want to capture visitors (so we haven't excluded them from being tagged). These usually include:

- Email Unsubscribe Page – OK, so they don't want your emails, but they might still be interested in buying.
- Complaints Page – this is one whose viewers you might want to exclude from seeing your ads.
- Order Confirmation Page – you may want to exclude people who've just ordered. Or – if you know customers buy once a month – hold onto them to show the ads at the right time.
- Delivery Information Page – could be hot prospects, maybe ones to send a Free P&P offer to.
- Wish Lists – again possibly hot prospects.
- Wedding List – if you offer special services like wedding lists or personal shopping – those page viewers deserve tailored ads.
- Checkout Pages – if you've lots of traffic, it's possible to target people who've reached the checkout, but not yet purchased.

These are just a selection of ideas for how viewers of different pages might be worth treating differently.

And we haven't even talked products yet! So let us do that. Taking remarketing to the nth degree would be creating an audience for each product and ads for each product too. Do not start there. In fact, don't even aim to get there in year one. For good reason:

- Remember – you need 100 people in a list before ads show; few sites have enough traffic to gather 100 people quickly at a product level.
- Think how much time it's going to take to set that up – will it ever be worth it? And the time to optimise it all!

So where should we go with product pages and our audience targeting?

There are two segmentation options (and you might want to do both):

- Site Depth
  People go through your site from Homepage, down to Category Page, down to Product List Page, down to Product Page. So you can segment based on how deep they get.

- Navigation Structure
  You have different categories of products – so maybe target by category: one audience for Kitchenware, another for Bathroom stuff. Remember: you are trying to segment your potential customers based on the pages they view.

After examining all of these possibilities, you will end up with an Audience Targeting Strategy that looks something like this:

Group of pages	Ad Message	Monthly page views
Whole site excluding order confirmation	Straight forward brand reminder, inc. key promotion	49,500
Wedding List	Set up your wedding list	100
Basket Pages	Test Brand Reminder, vs. Free Delivery offer	1,000
Delivery Information Pages	Test Brand Reminder, vs. Free Delivery offer	20
Mugs	Mugs advert	10,000

You'll see I've added a column for monthly page views – this gives you an idea of how many people you'll be able to get into that audience. The Delivery Information Pages is a great idea. But with only 20 views per month, it's not going to work. It will take you 5 months to get enough page views to show ads and the power of all remarketing is in how quickly you get it in front of the customer, so this is far too slow.

Step 4 – Get the lists and ads set up

Now you know what your Audience Targeting Strategy is, you can build your lists and the adgroups and adverts that will use them and drive the results.

To create a remarketing audience list, go to the "Shared Library" (in the left-hand menu in AdWords). A remarketing audience list is a definition of an audience. There are three types of audience you can use:

- Remarketing Tag-based – gathers all who looked at the tagged pages with a cookie.
- Remarketing Rule-based – uses the data gathered by a "Remarketing Tag-Based" list to form your audience, based on rules around the URLs people visited.

- Custom Combination – you select your audience based on whether it is/isn't in various other audience lists.

  When creating custom combinations, you're not limited to your URL and tag-based audience lists. You can also use Interest Categories (I suggest you ignore these until you've done the rest of your optimisation):

  All the lists have these settings:

  - Membership duration – see tip box
  - List definition – see below
  - Initial list size – see below

  NOTE: you can target ads purely at the interest categories – BUT these are not going to be as effective as your tag-based remarketing lists.

Most of what you set up will be using the custom combination, so it's a good idea to map it all out before you start and to give each list a good name and description so it's easy to remember who it's targeting. For example:

- Tag-Based = whole site tagged (excluding homepage)
- Rule-Based 1 = visited order confirmation page
- Rule-Based 2 = visited a product page
- **used to display ads** Rule-Based 3 = visited the catalogue request confirmation page
- Rule-Based 4 = visited the basket and checkout process (not including the order confirmation page)
- **used to display ads** Custom Combination 1 = {Rule-Based 2} AND DID NOT {Rule-Based 1}
- **used to display ads** Custom Combination 2 = {Rule-Based 4} AND DID NOT {Rule-Based 1}

Top Tip
Membership Duration

In Google remarketing, the membership duration is how long people will stay in that remarketing list after they last visited your website. So if they come again, they go back to day one. Membership duration is a really important thing to get right because:

- Make them too long and you will be showing your ads to people who last visited your site months ago, so the power of remarketing fades out.
- Make them too short and you won't get enough people for your ads to display. Remember you need 100 in any list – so you might not have enough traffic to get very involved with membership duration.

Once all the lists are set up, you can start on the adgroups.

First, create a new campaign to run this all through and check all the settings are right (see above on PPC for more detail on this). Don't forget to set the frequency capping (see tip box).

Then create an adgroup for each remarketing audience you will be targeting. Your ads will only be showing on the content network – so don't add any keywords.

Navigate into the adgroup and go into the Display Network tab. Here you can add your remarketing audience lists.

Your remarketing adverts will be appearing on the content network – here each website owner chooses what size space they are going to make available for adverts. They also choose what type of ads they are going to allow: image, text, or video, etc. To avoid excluding yourself from the site and to have the best chance of success, you want to be using as many of the ad formats as possible.

Top Tip
Frequency Capping

If you mention remarketing to someone 9 times out of 10 they talk of being "followed" or "haunted" around the internet by a company. That's because that company has left their frequency cap too high.

The frequency cap controls how many times per day your remarketing ads appear for each person on your list. It's set at the campaign level.

So put all your remarketing activity into just one campaign in Google Adwords so you're in total control of the maximum number of ads per day. Then initially set the cap to 5 per day and increase or decrease it as you need to.

As a minimum, make sure you're using text ads – they fit all spaces. Once you are using images, start with every size and see which works best for you.

Step 5 – Launch it

As soon as you have your campaign and your adverts set up, put it live. It might take a few more weeks for there to be 100 people in each list you're targeting, but as soon as there are 100 the ads will start.

How to optimise your remarketing

Key things to remember when optimising and analysing your remarketing activity are:

1. You are optimising people
2. You are not optimising the websites those people are looking at

So do not (until you have done the rest of the optimisation, anyway) exclude websites from your remarketing activity (unless they are sites you wouldn't want your brand to appear on, such as 'adult' sites).

That leaves you with these key areas you can change to improve performance and these are the areas you want to focus your optimisation on.

Optimisation option	What/How to test
Adverts – message	What messages work best for you? What offers work well?
Bids	How much are you happy to pay to make sure your ads are appearing?
Audience Structure	How can you better segment your visitors by collecting them into different lists? You may well find yourself creating ads that relate to individual product categories – so you can advertise men's clothes to those who have visited the men's pages.
Demographics	Which age ranges respond best? Are there some you want to exclude from Day one? (e.g. the under-18s?)
Cookie Lengths	How long after they have been to your site is it still worth showing someone your remarketing ads? (see also Cookie Top Tips)
Geographic	Some areas of the country will buy more from you than others – so this can be useful.
Managed Placements	There may be a handful of sites on the content network that perform better in remarketing for you – those sites that talk about your product, so you know your customer is thinking about the correct things when your ad appears. These will be worth turning into Managed Placements so you can bid higher to make sure you appear more often.
Frequency Capping	This is a general display network setting, set at Campaign level. It restricts how many times your ads are seen by people. You can do that per day, month, week and at Campaign, adgroup, or even individual ad level.

So although our favourite PPC keywords and placements can't be optimised in remarketing, there is a lot we can optimise.

When Doesn't Remarketing Work?

If you can't get the tracking code on your website (e.g. because you are PiggyBacking), then you are not going to be able to use remarketing. There are also a number of business sectors that are restricted from using remarketing, because the content of their sites means they're learning things about people we're not legally allowed to learn. This includes sensitive information such as racial, ethnic, political, sexual, dating, etc. If you think this might be you – check out the regulations on Google's site. In every other scenario, remarketing should work, as long as your numbers stack up. And if the numbers don't because your traffic is low – then it's just going to be a slower optimisation process. This is provided you can afford to get people to the website for the first time and then get them back again via remarketing without it becoming unprofitable. The only way to find that out is to try it, measure it, and optimise it.

What to Measure in Remarketing

Campaign	Impressions	Clicks	CTR%	Cost	Cost per Click	Orders	Value	AOV	Conversion Rate	Cost/ Sales
A	50,000	1,500	3%	555	37p	30	2,100	70	2%	26.4%
B	40,000	400	1%	180	45p	12	540	45	3%	33.3%

Below are the key metrics you need to be measuring for your remarketing; most are in the table above and they are very similar to PPC marketing:

- Impressions
- Clicks
- CTR %
- Cost
- Cost per Click
- Orders
- Sales
- AOV
- Conversion Rate
- Cost/Sales
- View-Through Conversions

For more information on each of these metrics, see Chapter 10. Use these metrics to compare the performance of your remarketing activity overall, and for any targeted campaigns you have underway.

. . . .

Successful Remarketing Checklist

- Know how much you can afford to spend to get each sale (your Cost/Sales).
- Spend time on your Audience Targeting Strategy.
- Start broad and then go more targeted.
- Test, test, test.
- Regularly review the results.

NOTES

What are the key points from this section?

_____

_____

_____

_____

_____

Other Notes:

_____

_____

_____

_____

_____

_____

WEBSITE

At the time of writing, remarketing is still a relatively new tool, so please visit **eCommerceMasterPlan.com** for the latest information on how remarketing can work for you.

9 Partnership Marketing

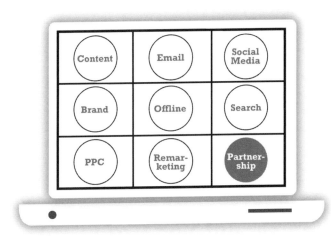

Partnership marketing is all about partnering with other organisations in a back-scratching way. The organisations you partner with should be targeting the same customer base as you, but offering something different.

Partnership agreements tend to involve swapping lists, or marketing space – and we'll look at the different options here.

GRADUATES

This method is particularly useful for these **eCommerce Business Structures**:

- Mail Order
- Full Multichannel

Partnership marketing works well for all **Product Range Scales** – but the more niche you are, the more partners you should be able to find!

It is also particularly useful if your **USPs** are:

- Customer Base – in most partnerships, you are trading access to your customer base – so the larger and better that is, the more successful you will be at finding partners.
- Brand – partnerships are most successful when the two companies involved appeal to the same sort of customers, so a clear brand really helps identify compatible partners.

Why Should You Use Partnerships if You Are an eCommerce Business?

Partnership marketing covers a wide range of options. It is not right for every eCommerce business, but when it works it can be a cheap and reliable way to recruit good-quality new customers. It's also a great way to increase brand awareness. The power of partnerships comes from the following:

- In any partnership arrangement, you are allying your brand with another business's brand – so you can increase the power of your brand if you choose the right partners.
- You can target specific customer groups – by picking the right partners, you will be targeting consumers who are highly likely to be interested in your products.
- It should always be profitable – often partnerships are "free", so there is a straightforward swap of opportunities. At worst, they are priced on success – a commission on sales, or a fixed fee per activity. So you are in control of any costs and they should be low.
- They are a great way to target and recruit new customers and get them buying from you.

Partnership Marketing Objectives for eCommerce Businesses

Partnership activity should be purely focused on recruiting new customers. And it should be a low-cost way to do that.

That will come from making sure you are working with the right partners: those who support and help build your brand.

How Partnership Marketing Works

Put simply, partnership marketing is two (or more) businesses agreeing to do some joint marketing, or swap access to their customers. The businesses you partner with don't have to be eCommerce businesses; you might decide to partner with a magazine, blog, or charity – anyone who wants to speak to the same consumers as you.

Key types of partnerships

Partnership marketing has been around in the mail-order world for decades, with companies swapping mailing lists or inserts (catalogues to put in each other's parcels). But it has been slow to catch on in the online world – surprising, considering how much easier, cheaper and lower risk it is to use partnerships online than offline.

These are the most common methods of partnership for eCommerce businesses, but they are certainly not the only options – these are only limited by you and your partners' imaginations.

Parcel bouncebacks

A bounceback is marketing literature put in the parcel that delivers the goods to the customer. (You should already be putting your own marketing into your parcels.) With a partnership, you agree to swap a defined number of items (usually a catalogue or flyer) with another business. You put theirs in your parcels and they put your marketing material in their parcels.

Don't forget to check how fast they'll get through the marketing materials – you don't want all theirs out within two weeks and yours taking two months to get out – it needs to be more even than that.

Order confirmation email bouncebacks

This uses the same principle as for the parcel bouncebacks, only this time you include a banner or link to your partner in your order confirmation emails.

Order confirmation page bounceback

This can be really powerful – as soon as someone's bought from you, you show them an advert for your partner.

It's particularly good because (i) they have already bought from you today, so you're not going to worry about sending them somewhere else, (ii) they are in a buying mood, so should be a good prospect for your partner.

Email advertising swaps

This is when you each agree to send an email about the other to your database.

So you send an email to your list recommending your partner and they send one to their list recommending you. It could be a whole email, or it might just be a banner.

Make sure that you are both sending to a similar volume and also quality, of people – you don't want to be sent to their enquirer list if you are sending them to your best buyers.

Website advertising

You each put a banner for the other on your website. Don't forget to agree how long it will be up for and where.

Social media mentions

This could be blog posts, tweets, retweets, Facebook competitions, or more. As the power in social media comes from engagement, partnering for social media shares can be **very** helpful.

WORKBOOK

To help you get your partnerships set up, we have created a handy workbook. Download it from the website: **eCommerceMasterPlan.com/Free**

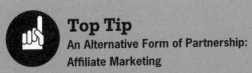

Top Tip
An Alternative Form of Partnership:
Affiliate Marketing

Affiliate marketing is a method of offering any website a commission on sales they send to you. Generally, it's a very broad piece of activity: you let anyone advertise you, so you are letting go of control over where you appear.

While a lot of affiliates are people who have websites on a certain topic that they are looking to monetise, there are also a lot of voucher code sites, cashback sites and other highly unfocused affiliates.

To tap into this massive marketplace, you need to use one of the big affiliate networks. They have all the software and deal with all the money and give you access to thousands of website owners who may want to advertise your products.

Unlike normal partnering, you don't have much control over what customers are driven to you; with some of my mail-order clients, I have found that over 70% of all people buying via the affiliates channel were already our customers. So it can also be expensive. You will pay a monthly fee to the network, a commission to the affiliates of 5–15% and a further 3–4% of all sales to the network too.

If you have a product that's attractive to many people, this can be a very quick way to generate sales and build your business.

How to set up a partnership

There are two key things that make a successful partnership marketing campaign:

- The two partners have similar brand values and target the same customers. For example, Screwfix and New Look wouldn't work, but Boden and Waitrose would.
- There has to be enough in it for both parties, but what's in it for both might not be the same thing. You might swap inserts for social media.

If you are interested in getting a partnership up and running, you first need to identify who you would like to partner with. Which brands do your customers also like? Who do they also shop with? A simple way to find that out is to ask them! Just run a survey to find out where else they shop. (SurveyMonkey is a great tool for this.)

Once you have identified which businesses you want to partner with (and I'd aim to have a list of at least 10) you need to get in contact with them. Call them, email them, DM them on Twitter, send them a letter, connect on LinkedIn – it can take a while to get to them and to the right person.

It is crucial to get the first contact right: be friendly and not pushy, because the person you're approaching might not be aware of the partnership concept – you may need to convince them it's a good one and that it won't annoy their customers. Use some examples of other people who are already doing it, if you have previously done it, show them the results. It can take a long time to build up the relationship to the point they're happy to do the deal.

Plus, before you start discussions, make sure you have a clear idea of what you can offer and what you would like from them in return.

If everyone's happy, make sure you get everything in writing. You don't necessarily need to go to the lawyers, but make sure there is a document you are all in agreement on. Include all the details: time scales, what's being done, volumes, tracking codes, etc. When partners fall out, it's almost guaranteed to have been because someone assumed something was agreed that wasn't – so make sure you're all clear on all the details.

Then you can get on with the activity. Once done, don't forget to review the results – and see if it's worked well for them too. If it has, you should be able to get them to agree to continue with it, or expand the relationship and try something else.

Partnerships are all about building up a trusting, fair relationship with another business in order to create benefits for you both. Not all partnerships will work – so make sure you're always working on new agreements with new partners.

. . . .

When Doesn't Partnership Marketing Work?

In one form or another, partnership marketing can work for any business, of any size, in any marketplace (not just eCommerce). Partnerships are everywhere and if you follow the process above and find the right partners, they will work for you, too.

When it doesn't work is when you can't find companies willing to partner with you, but you won't know if that's the case until you start trying.

What to Measure in Partnership Marketing

Partnership Tactic	Visits	Bounce Rate	Orders	Value	AOV	Conversion Rate	Sales/ Visit
X Email	5,000	30%	26	1,820	70	5%	36.4p
Y Conf Page	5,000	35%	35	1,575	45	8%	31.5p

Below are the key metrics you need to be measuring for your partnership marketing; most are in the table above. Different pieces of partnership activity will come in at different speeds. An email will be done within a week, whereas an order confirmation link may be in place for 12 months – so be sure to compare results fairly.

- Visits
- Bounce Rate
- Orders
- Conversion Rate
- Sales
- AOV
- Sales per Visitor

For more information on each of these metrics, see Chapter 10.

....

Successful Partnership Marketing Checklist

- Have clear objectives
- Select the companies to partner with carefully

- Make sure you deliver on your end of the bargain
- Keep looking for new opportunities
- Be creative!

NOTES

What are the key points from this section?

_____

_____

_____

_____

Who could you partner with?

_____

_____

_____

_____

Other Notes:

_____

_____

_____

_____

WEBSITE
Visit **eCommerceMasterPlan.com** for the latest information on partnership marketing.

CHAPTER 10

The Metrics

· ·

At the end of each chapter, we've listed the metrics you need to measure that marketing method. In this final chapter, you'll find an explanation of what each one is and, where possible, benchmarks for it. One of the things I'm asked very often is what the benchmarks are for various metrics – so I hope this will prove useful!

After much deliberating, the metrics are in an A–Z order!

AOV, Average Order Value

What is it?
The average order value
Sales divided by orders

Benchmarks
Partly depends on what you are promoting. But generally you should benchmark against the AOV of the whole site.

Attempted

What is it?
The number of emails you tried to send

Bounce Rate

What is it?
A percentage

A bounce is someone who arrives on your website, looks at the page they landed on, and then leaves. It's a good indicator of whether you're driving quality traffic and of the quality of your landing pages.

Benchmarks
A bounce rate below what your website achieves on average is good. If it's as low as 30% you have nothing to worry about.

Brand Recall

What is it?
Gathered through surveys of the target market. It will show how effectively the advertising has made people more aware of your brand.

Clicks

What is it?
How many times your marketing was clicked on, especially relevant for email and PPC.

Click Rate

What is it?
A percentage used in email marketing
Clicked divided by opened

Benchmarks
This should be over 25%. Most importantly, look at where yours usually is and take note if it changes.

CTR, Click-Through Rate

What is it?
A percentage used in PPC and remarketing
Clicks divided by impressions
This shows how attractive your ads are to those who you have put them in front of.

Benchmarks
This will vary, depending on the targeting of the activity.
In search PPC, expect it to be between 1 and 10%. If you are bidding on your brand name, it will probably be in double figures.
If your activity is also on the content network then CTR will be lower.
In social media PPC, expect it to be a fraction of a per cent.

Conversion Rate

What is it?
A percentage
Orders divided by clicks, or visits

Benchmarks
A conversion rate above what your website achieves on average is good.

Cost

What is it?
How much it costs
Remember to include everything – the cost of the data, the print, the photography, etc.

Cost per 1,000 Impressions

What is it?
Cost divided by impressions

Benchmarks
Enables you to compare the relative costs of different advertising.

Cost per Item

What is it?
Cost divided by items distributed. Mainly used in direct mail.

Benchmarks
Compare with other activity – and the impact it creates. Is it worth it?

Cost/Profit per Order

What is it?
(Sales minus cost) divided by orders. This enables you to compare all the offline activity (and online activity) you are doing.

Benchmarks
What do you need it to be?

Cost/Sales (see p. 123)

What is it?
A percentage
Cost as a percentage of the sales
Cost divided by sales

Benchmarks
For a brand adgroup, this should be very small – under 5%.
For the rest, you need to be willing to spend between 20 and 40% of the sales on clicks.

CPC, Cost Per Click

What is it?
Cost divided by clicks

Delivered

What is it?
The number of emails that were actually delivered

Delivery rate

What is it?
A percentage
Delivered divided by attempted

Benchmarks
If it's not over 90%, you need to clean your data better or change your hosting and software.

Distributed

What is it?
The number of items you have distributed in that way. Catalogues or direct mail sent, copies of the magazine, etc.

Email sign-up

What is it?
The number of people who sign up to receive your emails.

Benchmarks
Track month to month and see how much you can grow it.

Impressions

What is it?
How many eyeballs did your advertising get in front of?

No. of X driving the traffic

What is it?
For traffic from search engines, this would be the number of keywords.

This gives you a view on the visibility you are getting in the search results.

Benchmarks
Basically, you just want to keep seeing this number getting higher.

Open Rate

What is it?
A percentage used in email marketing
Opened divided by delivered

Benchmarks
This should be over 25%. Most importantly, look at where yours usually is and take note if it changes.

Opened

What is it?
The number of recipients who opened your email

Orders

What is it?
The number of orders placed as a result of the activity

Response Rate

What is it?
A percentage
Orders divided by distributed

Benchmarks
Compare with other activity – what do you need to be getting?

Sales

What is it?
The value of the orders placed

Sales per Delivered

What is it?
A great way to compare the performance of emails when the list size varies
Sales divided by delivered

Benchmarks
After a few emails, you will see where this should be for your business – so keep an eye out for those emails/segments that under- or over-perform.

Sales per Visitor

What is it?
Sales divided by visitors
A great way to compare the performance of activity where the traffic volume varies

Sign-ups

What is it?
If there's a call to action in the advertising – how many people did it? It might be to sign up for emails, follow on Facebook, or take advantage of an offer.

Unsubscribes

What is it?
The number of recipients who unsubscribe

Unsubscribe Rate

What is it?
A percentage
Unsubscribes divided by delivered

Benchmarks
Every email will get unsubscribes. Normally this will be around 1%.
Don't worry until it hits 2 or 3%.

View-Through Conversions

What is it?
The number of orders placed by people who've seen your remarketing
ads, but not clicked on them.

Benchmarks
Usually a lot higher than the number of conversions driven by
remarketing clicks.

Visits

What is it?
The number of visitors getting to your website, useful for comparing
traffic sources.

Benchmarks
There is no benchmark as such for this, but it should be increasing
month to month.

You've Read the Book, What's Next?

· ·

You have now learnt all about the nine key marketing methods for eCommerce, which businesses they should work with, how to do them, when they won't work, the objectives and the key metrics to track. Now it's time to start implementing. But it's not time to stop learning – eCommerce and online marketing are still evolving so:

- Always keep optimising – optimise your products, your website, your financials and, of course, your marketing.
- Keep learning – watch out for new opportunities and test those you think might work for your business.
- Download and use the workbooks for each marketing method that are available at **eCommerceMasterPlan.com/Free**

I am committed to keeping **eCommerceMasterPlan.com** up to date with the information the eCommerce business owner or marketer needs to know. It is simple, sensible advice. Visit today and subscribe to our emails and follow us on social media.

Most of all – enjoy it!

Chloë

P.S. please do let me know how you get on – I'd love to hear from you. Email me at chloe@eCommerceMasterPlan.com

If you want more help, or want to accelerate your progress even faster...

- Chloë is available to speak or consult right now – contact details below
- Look out for the eCommerce MasterPlan Marketing workshops
- Read my first book *eCommerce MasterPlan: Your 3 Steps to Successful Online Selling* to find out how to build your eCommerce business for growth
- On the website we have details of where Chloë is speaking in the coming months
- Chloë's online marketing agency, indiumonline, can help you with a range of managed online marketing activity, see indiumonline.co.uk
- Plus you'll find lots of great extra content on **eCommerceMasterPlan.com**
- Watch out for further eCommerce MasterPlan books, available at **eCommerceMasterPlan.com/Books**

Contact Details:

t: 01865 980 616 or 01872 888 737

e: chloe@ecommercemasterplan.com

Praise for *eCommerce MasterPlan*

. . . .

'Chloë has done the impossible – condensed a massively complex and detailed subject into a crisp, clear set of "To Do" lists with masses of live examples. I tried very hard, but could not find anything she had left out.

Anyone running an eCommerce business will relate to so much of this book and get the inspiration to get on and improve their business almost immediately.

In 12 years of running an eCommerce business, I have found that just as you crack one new method of digital marketing, two more grow in its place. This book seems to get a grip of all the methods and allows you to conquer them in a manageable way.

If you are just starting on the eCommerce route, congratulations, you have found the Bible – I suggest you read Step 2 (How to build the right website) very thoroughly, right now!'

Mark Ashley Miller, Founder, The Present Finder

'This is the Bible to Website Management and Marketing 101. A good bookshelf addition for all dot.com dinosaurs, successful online managers, web entrepreneurs, or total novices who need a no-nonsense, straight-to-the-point read of where to start and how.

I myself have been in this industry now for twelve years and it's always good to go back to the basics and refresh your own learning – that's why I love this book.

Chloë Thomas shows you step by step how to build and manage your online business. She strips back to the core of what you are trying to achieve and demonstrates that it takes work, but it's much easier than you thought. Easy and enjoyable to read, with a clear plan of action and totally applicable to today.'

Maxine Duncan, Online Commercial Manager, La Senza UK

'eCommerce can be a minefield of abbreviations, technical terms, and (like IT) a complex journey that would scare most people off creating and marketing a website.

The *eCommerce MasterPlan* by Chloë, an experienced eCommerce professional, breaks down many of the uncertainties of the eCommerce world. Understanding your business model as identified in Step 1 is key and following the simple worksheets will really set you up for success and help you plan properly.

Throughout the *eCommerce MasterPlan*, relevance is put on the importance of content being King. Plus, one small step that is planned is better than jumping in feet first with multiple ideas that don't get the attention needed. Chloë has also laid bare the fundamentals of running a website, going out to tender with documents to make life easier and the key components of driving traffic to a website.

This book has something for everyone, whether a novice entering the world of eCommerce or someone like myself who has worked in eCommerce for many years. There is a takeaway for everyone.

This eCommerce master class not only covers the core elements you would expect but goes one step further; highlighting how to work out ROI, and giving simple examples that actually make sense. Plus, it's packed with ideas that you will be able to apply to your everyday planning, implementation and review of digital marketing.

A great read and followed up by a training course that will keep your mind bubbling for hours to come.'

Lee Carpenter-Johnson, E-commerce Director, Galactic Online

'The *eCommerce MasterPlan* provides a useful roadmap for what is still a relatively new industry. The MasterPlan has a first step to assist the reader in identifying their type of business and removes any concern of a "one size fits all" approach. The author has used her broad experience to provide a book giving the sort of specialised advice normally only available with large-scale consulting spend.

This book is a must-read for anyone looking to build on their eCommerce efforts. The added content online gives the reader the chance to work examples, complete workbooks, as well as the comfort that this is as up to date as the author's impressive knowledge base.'

P. Cuthbert, Project Manager, Tesco.com

PHILIP'

CW00405699

STRE

Leicester

and Loughborough

www.philips-maps.co.uk

First published in 2008 by

Philip's, a division of
Octopus Publishing Group Ltd
www.octopusbooks.co.uk
2-4 Heron Quays, London E14 4JP
An Hachette Livre UK Company

First edition 2008
First impression 2008

ISBN 978-0-540-09202-4

© Philip's 2008

Ordnance Survey®

This product includes mapping data licensed
from Ordnance Survey®, with the
permission of the Controller of Her Majesty's
Stationery Office.© Crown copyright 2008.
All rights reserved.
Licence number 100011710

Data for the speed cameras provided by
PocketGPSWorld.com Ltd.

Ordnance Survey and the OS symbol are
registered trademarks of Ordnance Survey,
the national mapping agency of Great Britain

Photographic acknowledgements:
VIII Ian Francis / Alamy
IX Colin Palmer Photography / Alamy

Printed by Toppan, China

Contents

Key to map symbols

Roads

(12)	Motorway with junction number
A42	Primary route – dual, single carriageway
A42	A road – dual, single carriageway
B1289	B road – dual, single carriageway
	Through-route – dual, single carriageway
	Minor road – dual, single carriageway
	Rural track, private road or narrow road in urban area
	Path, bridleway, byway open to all traffic, road used as a public path
	Road under construction
	Pedestrianised area
	Gate or obstruction to traffic restrictions may not apply at all times or to all vehicles
P P&R	Parking, Park and Ride
(30) (30)	Speed cameras – single, multiple

Railways

	Railway
	Miniature railway
	Metro station, private railway station

Emergency services

Ambulance station, coastguard station

Fire station, police station

H ✚ Hospital, Accident and Emergency entrance to hospital

General features

✚ PO   Place of worship, Post Office

i   Information centre (open all year)

Bus or coach station, shopping centre

Important buildings, schools, colleges, universities and hospitals

Woods, built-up area

Tumulus FORT   Non-Roman antiquity, Roman antiquity

Leisure facilities

Camping site, caravan site

Golf course, picnic site

Boundaries

| • • • • • • • | Postcode boundaries |
| —— · —— | County and unitary authority boundaries |

Water features

River Ouse Tidal water, water name

Non-tidal water – lake, river, canal or stream

‹ ┃ Lock, weir

Enlarged mapping only

Railway or bus station building

Place of interest

Parkland

Scales

Blue pages: 4½ inches to 1 mile 1:14 080

| 0 | 220 yds | ¼ mile | 660 yds | ½ mile |

| 0 | 125m | 250m | 375m | ½ km |

Red pages: 7 inches to 1 mile 1:9051

| 0 | 110 yds | 220 yds | 330 yds | ¼ mile |

| 0 | 125m | 250m | 375m | ½km |

62 Adjoining page indicators The colour of the arrow and the band indicates the scale of the adjoining page (see above)

Abbreviations

Acad	Academy		Mkt	Market
Allot Gdns	Allotments		Meml	Memorial
Cemy	Cemetery		Mon	Monument
C Ctr	Civic Centre		Mus	Museum
CH	Club House		Obsy	Observatory
Coll	College		Pal	Royal Palace
Crem	Crematorium		PH	Public House
Ent	Enterprise		Recn Gd	Recreation Ground
Ex H	Exhibition Hall		Resr	Reservoir
Ind Est	Industrial Estate		Ret Pk	Retail Park
IRB Sta	Inshore Rescue Boat Station		Sch	School
			Sh Ctr	Shopping Centre
Inst	Institute		TH	Town Hall/House
Ct	Law Court		Trad Est	Trading Estate
L Ctr	Leisure Centre		Univ	University
LC	Level Crossing		Wks	Works
Liby	Library		YH	Youth Hostel

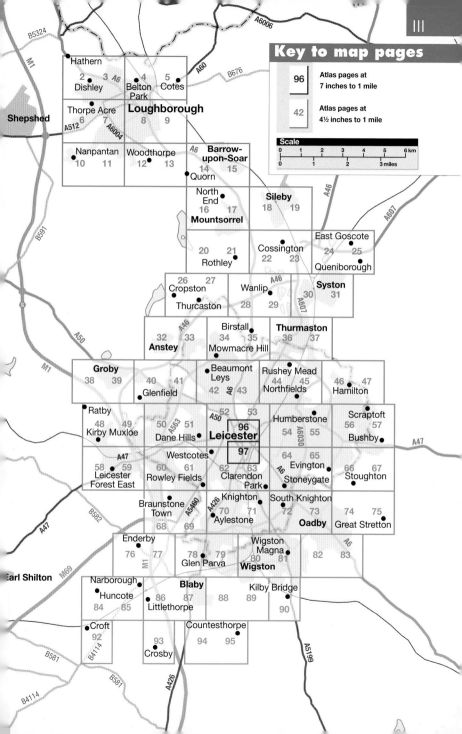

Key to map pages

| 96 | Atlas pages at 7 inches to 1 mile |
| 42 | Atlas pages at 4½ inches to 1 mile |

Scale

0 1 2 3 4 5 6 km
0 1 2 3 miles

B5324

M1

Hathern

2 Dishley 3 A6 4 Belton Park 5 Cotes

Thorpe Acre A512 6 7 A6004

Loughborough

8 9

Nanpantan 10 11 Woodthorpe 12 13

A6 **Barrow-upon-Soar**

14 Quorn 15

North End 16 17

Sileby 18 19

Mountsorrel

A6006

A60

B676

A46

A607

B591

B591

20 21 Rothley

Cossington 22 23

East Goscote 24 25

Queniborough

26 27 Cropston

Thurcaston

Wanlip 28 29

A46 30 **Syston** 31

A607

A50

M1

32 33 **Anstey**

Birstall 34 35 Mowmacre Hill

Thurmaston 36 37

Groby 38 39

40 41 Glenfield

Beaumont Leys 42 A6 43

Rushey Mead 44 45 Northfields

46 47 Hamilton

Ratby 48 49 Kirby Muxloe

50 A563 51 Dane Hills

A50 52 53

Leicester 96 97

Humberstone 54 A6030 55

Scraptoft 56 57 Bushby

A47

A47 58 59 Leicester Forest East

Westcotes 60 61 Rowley Fields

62 63 Clarendon Park

64 65 Evington Stoneygate

A6

66 67 Stoughton

Braunstone Town 68 69

A5460 A426 Knighton 70 71 Aylestone

South Knighton 72 73 **Oadby**

74 75 Great Stretton

Enderby 76 77

M1 78 79 Glen Parva

Wigston Magna 80 81 **Wigston**

A6 82 83

Earl Shilton

M69 B582

A47 B582

Narborough Huncote 84 85

Blaby 86 87 Littlethorpe

88 89 Kilby Bridge

90

A5199

Croft 92 B4114

93 Crosby

Countesthorpe 94 95

A426

B581

B581

B4114

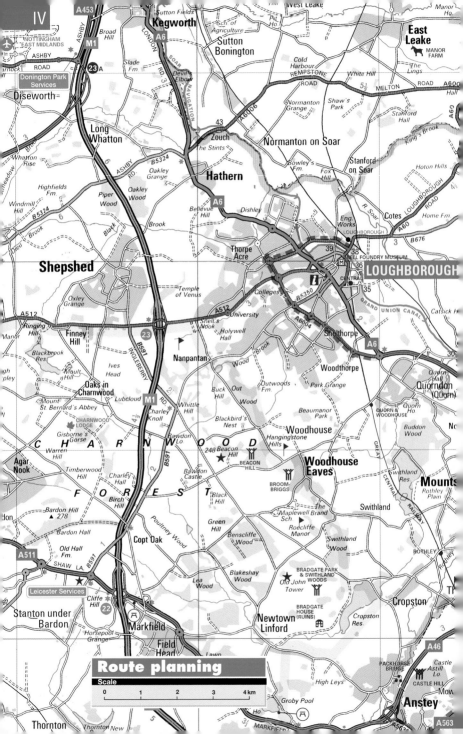

Route planning

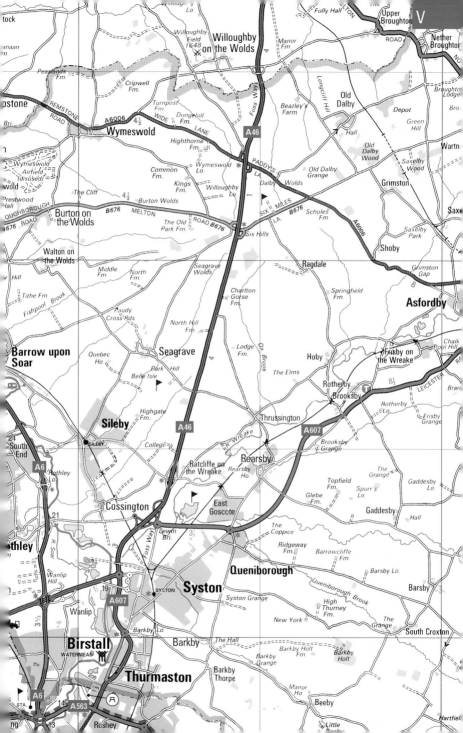

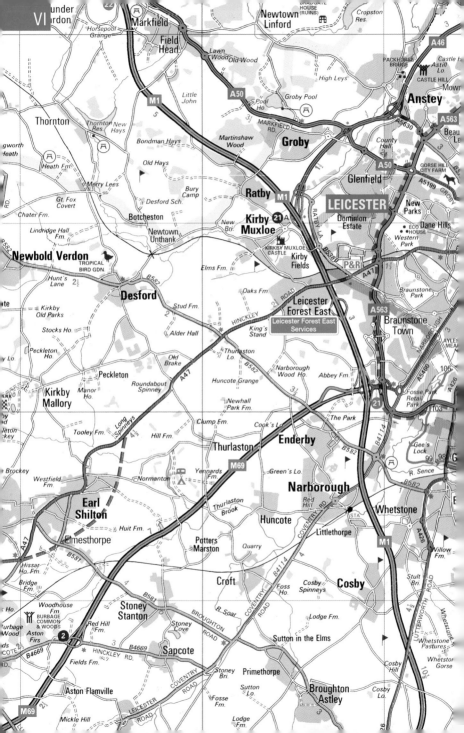

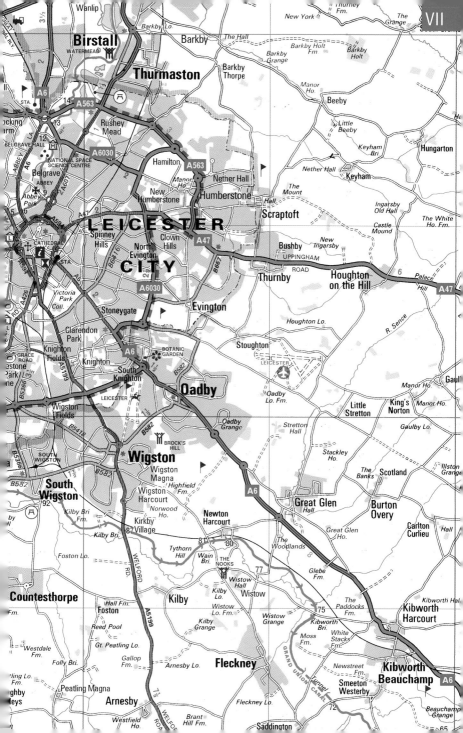

Visitor attractions

Museums and Galleries

Abbey Pumping Station Museum *Corporation Road, Leicester* A museum of science and technology, exploring the history of steam and industry over the last 200 years. Exhibitions on light, transport and public health. ☎0116 299 5111 🖥www.leicestermuseums.ac.uk 43 B2

Belgrave Hall Museum & Gardens *Church Road, Belgrave, Leicester* The period rooms contrast the lives of those who lived there in the 18th century. The Community Gallery illustrates the history of the area with the gardens dating from the 1850s. ☎0116 266 6590 🖥www.leicestermuseums.ac.uk 43 C3

Charles Moore Collection of Musical Instruments *Music Department, University Road, Leicester* Specialising in 18th and 19th century woodwind and brass instruments, with archives of musical material. ☎0116 252 2781 🖥www.le.ac.uk 97 C1

The City Gallery *Granby Street, opp Dover Street, Leicester* Contemporary art gallery with fine art and crafts from the region. 🖥www.leicester.gov.uk/citygallery ☎0116 223 2067 97 C3

The Guildhall *Guildhall Lane, Leicester* This 14th century building was opened as a museum in 1926. The museum displays local history and Victorian police cells and is reputedly the city's most haunted building. ☎0116 253 2569 🖥www.leicestermuseums.ac.uk 96 A3

Guru Nanak Sikh Museum *9 Holy Bones* First Sikh museum in UK. ☎0116 262 8606 🖥www.thesikhmuseum.com 96 A4

▼ *The National Space Centre*

Jewry Wall Museum *St Nicholas Circle, Leicester* A museum of archaeology located in Roman public baths. It holds the remains of Roman walling with mosaics and portraits of the city throughout its history. ☎0116 225 4971

John Taylor Bellfoundry Museum *Freehold Street, Loughborough* Exhibits and memorabilia of this industry. Tours are available. ☎01509 233414 🖥www.taylorbells.co.uk 8 C4

New Walk Museum & Art Gallery *New Walk, Leicester* The city's oldest museum, it displays natural history with exhibitions such as Wild Space, The Mighty Dinosaurs, Ancient Egyptians and World Arts. Temporary exhibitions and coffee shop. 🖥www.leicestermuseums.ac.uk ☎0116 225 4900 97 C2

Newarke Houses Museum *The Newarke, Leicester* Telling the story of Leicester with World War I reconstructions of trenches and street scenes. Tudor toy collection, drapers shop and a costume museum. 🖥www.leicestermuseums.ac.uk ☎0116 225 4980 97 A3

The Old Rectory *Rectory Place, Loughborough* The building dates from 1228 and displays collections from the history of the surrounding area, including archaeological finds. ☎01509 634704 🖥www.loughborough.co.uk 8 B4

Royal Infirmary Museum *Knighton Street, Leicester* Displays photographs and artefacts from the history of the hospital. Medicine bottles, stoneware and surgical equipment on display. 🖥www.lri.org.uk ☎0116 254 1414 97 B2

War Memorial Museum *Granby Street, Loughborough* A tower with three floors of wartime objects and the history of the airborne forces. It was built as a memorial for the Great War and contains 47 bells. 🖥www.loughboroughcarillon.com ☎01509 263370 8 A4

Historic Sites

Clock Tower *East Gates, Leicester* Constructed in 1868 for traffic control, it boasts a statue of a son of Leicester in each corner. 🖥www.leicester.gov.uk ☎0116 257 1080 96 B4

Kirby Muxloe Castle *Kirby Muxloe, Leicester* Picturesque ruins of a fortified manor house dating from 1480. 🖥www.english-heritage.org.uk ☎0116 238 6886 48 C2

Leicester Abbey *Abbey Park, Abbey Park Road, Leicester* The ruined Abbey of St Mary de Pratis, which was founded as a community of Augustinian Canons in 1143. 🖥www.leicester.gov.uk ☎0116 222 1000 53 A4

Leicester Castle *Castle Yard, Leicester* An important monument centred around Castle Yard. The Great Hall is medieval with original woodwork from 1150. 🖥www.leicestermuseums.ac.uk ☎0116 253 2569 97 A3

The Magazine Gateway *The Newarke, Leicester* Built around 1400, these stone walls once surrounded a church, hospital and priests houses. It was also used as a store for weapons in the Civil War. 🖥www.leicestermuseums.ac.uk 97 A3

Places of Worship

Leicester Cathedral *St Martin's, Leicester* A church has been on this site since 1086. It contains a memorial to Richard III and memorials to those in the World Wars. Visitor centre with a café. 🖥www.cathedral.leicester.anglican.org ☎0116 248 7400 96 B3

St Mary de Castro *Castle View, Leicester* Built in the early 12th century, it has a needle spire, chancel and was the scene of the knighting of Henry VI. 🖥www.leicester.gov.uk ☎0116 262 8727 97 A3

St Nicholas *St Nicholas' Circle, Leicester* The oldest church in Leicester contains two anglo-saxon window openings. Roman pillars remain in the churchyard. 🖥www.stnicholasleicester.com ☎0116 248 7471 96 A3

All Saints *High Cross Street, Leicester* A Norman church dating from 13th century, containing a tomb recess and a mayor's chair from 18th century. 🖥www.leicester.gov.uk 96 A4

Green Spaces

Abbey Park *Abbey Park Road, Leicester* Leicester's main park is divided by the River Soar and has formal gardens, Chinese garden, ruins, bandstand, model railway, pets corner and a large children's play area. ☎0116 233 3028 🖥www.leicester.gov.uk 53 A4

Bede Park *Western Boulevard, Leicester* Modern park running alongside the old River Soar and Grand Union Canal. Contains a Mediterranean style plaza, several pieces of art and ornamental shrubs. 🖥www.leicester.gov.uk ☎0116 233 3028 97 A2

Braunstone Park *Gooding Avenue, Leicester* Surrounding Braunstone Hall, it has a mixture of woodland, spinneys, meadows and lakes. Also home to the Model Aircraft Club. ☎0116 233 3028 🖥www.leicester.gov.uk 61 A3

Brocks Hill Country Park *Washbrook Lane, Oadby* 67 acres of woodland, ponds and meadows. Visitor centre and café on site. 🖥www.oadby-wigston.gov.uk ☎0116 257 2888 82 A4

Castle Gardens *The Newarke, Leicester* Peaceful garden at Leicester's Castle.

Contains a rock garden, river boat landing and a picnic area. ☎0116 233 3028 🖥www.leicester.gov.uk 96 A3

Castle Hill Country Park *Leicester Road, off the A46, Leicester* More than 250 acres of grassland and woodland, along with a new apple orchard. ☎0116 233 3028 🖥www.leicester.gov.uk 33 A2

Evington Park *The Common, Evington* Large parkland filled with old oak and chestnut trees. The Black Mulberry tree was planted in 1836. Areas for bowls, tennis, football and cricket. ☎0116 233 3028 🖥www.leicester.gov.uk 65 B3

Humberstone Park *Uppingham Road, Humberstone* A 20-acre park with gardens and children's play area. Contains the Bushby Brook and the Rally Bank, a haven for wild plants and animals. ☎0116 233 3028🖥www.leicester.gov.uk 55 A3

Knighton Park *Kingsmead Road, Leicester* A 78-acre park with water garden, heather woodlands and a variety of sporting facilities. ☎0116 233 3028 🖥www.leicester.gov.uk 72 B2

Shady Lane Aboretum *Shady Lane, Evington* A popular city open space, with over 500 species of trees, rare wild flowers and river birds. ☎0116 233 3028 🖥www.leicester.gov.uk 65 C1

University of Leicester Botanic Garden *Stoughton Drive South, Oadby* Founded in 1921, the 16-acre gardens surround 4 houses, with herb and rock gardens, woodland, glasshouses and the Attenborough Arboretum. 🖥www.le.ac.uk/botanic garden ☎0116 271 2933 73 A3

Victoria Park *London Road, Leicester* Formerly the town's racecourse, today there is a pavilion, war memorials and flower displays. It is home to the annual Caribbean Carnival. ☎0116 233 3028 🖥www.leicester.gov.uk 63 C3

Watermead Country Park *Fillingate, Wanlip* Popular for walkers, cyclists and bird watchers, it has two lakes, sculptures and prehistoric remains. ☎0116 233 3028 🖥www.leics.gov.uk 29 C3

Western Park *Hinckley Road, Leicester* The largest park in Leicester, it has a mixture of meadows and mature woods, with children's play areas, bowling greens and woodland walks. ☎0116 233 3028 🖥www.leicester.gov.uk 51 A2

Other Activities

Aylestone Leisure Centre *Knighton Lane East, Leicester* Ball courts, sports hall, public swimming pool and soft play area for children. ☎0116 233 3040 🖥www.leicester.gov.uk/sports 71 A4

Braunstone Leisure Centre *Hamelin Road, Braunstone, Leicester* Swimming pool, fitness suites, badminton courts and outdoor play area. ☎0116 229 3229 🖥www.leicester.gov.uk/sports 51 A1

▲ *Leicester city centre*

De Montfort Hall *Granville Road, Leicester* This popular venue presents jazz, ballet, comedy, opera and West End musicals throughout the year. ☎0116 233 3111 🖥www.demontforthall.co.uk 63 C3

Gorse Hill City Farm *Anstey Lane, Leicester* A working farm with a variety of farmyard animals, as well as children's play area and café. 🖥www.gorsehillcityfarm.org.uk ☎0116 253 7582 42 A1

Great Central Railway *Great Central Station, Loughborough* A heritage railway that runs for 8 miles from Loughborough to the outskirts of Leicester. Visitors can drive trains and dine on board. 🖥www.gcrailway.co.uk ☎01509 230726 8 C3

The Haymarket Shopping Centre *Humberstone Gate, Leicester* Wide variety of shops under one roof. ☎0116 262 3774 🖥www.haymarketshopping.co.uk 96 B4

Haymarket Theatre *Halford Street, Leicester* This theatre forms part of the Leicester Theatre Trust with a performance arts centre. ☎0116 253 0021 🖥www.lhtheatre.co.uk 96 B4

Leicester City Football Club *The Walkers Stadium, Filbert Way, Leicester* The Foxes were founded in 1884 and play in the Championship. ☎0870 040 6000 / 499 1884 🖥www.lcfc.premiumtv.co.uk 62 C2

Leicester Market *Market Place, Leicester* From Monday to Saturday over 270 stalls sell local organic foods, clothes and jewellery. There has been a market here for the last 700 years. Also hosts a farmers market. 🖥www.leicester.gov.uk ☎0116 223 2376/7 96 B3

Leicester Racecourse *Leicester Road, Oadby* Horse racing venue with over 100 years history. Tours are available. 🖥www.leicester-racecourse.co.uk ☎0116 271 6515 72 C2

Leicester Tigers *Welford Road Stadium, Aylestone Road, Leicester* In existence since 1892, the 'Tigers' have been one of the most successful Guiness

Premiership teams. 🖥www.tigers.co.uk ☎0870 128 3430 97 B1

Leicestershire County Cricket Club County Ground, Grace Road, Leicester Opened in 1878, the ground has a museum and tours. ☎0871 282 1879 🖥www.leicestershireccc.com 70 C3

The Little Theatre *Dover Street, Leicester* Amateur theatre company showcasing dramas to pantomimes. The host for visiting drama companies and the youth theatre. 🖥www.thelittletheatre.net ☎0116 255 1302 97 C3

Meridian Leisure Park *Lubbesthorpe Way, Leicester* Ten pin bowling, cinema, leisure centre and restaurants. ☎0116 263 1234 🖥www.meridian-leisure.co.uk 60 C1

National Space Centre *Exploration Drive, Leicester* Award winning attraction with a futuristic rocket tower, space theatre, interactive exhibits and human spaceflight. Café and picnic area. 🖥www.spacecentre.co.uk ☎0870 607 7223 43 B2

Phoenix Arts Centre *Upper Brown Street, Leicester* Centre for film, music and theatre performances. ☎0116 224 7700 🖥www.phoenix.org.uk 97 B3

The Shires Shopping Centre *High Street, Leicester* More than 80 stores. ☎0116 251 2461 🖥www.theshires.co.uk 96 B4

Information

🛈 **Leicester Tourist Information Centre** *Every Street, Town Hall Square, Leicester* ☎0906 294 1113 96 B3

🛈 **Loughborough Tourist Information Centre** *Market Place, Loughborough* ☎01509 218113 8 B4

Leicester City Council *Marlborough Street* ☎0116 252 7000 🖥www.leicester.gov.uk 97 B3

Car Parking ☎0116 223 2148 🖥www.leicester.gov.uk

National Rail Enquiries ☎08457 484950 🖥www.nationalrail.co.uk

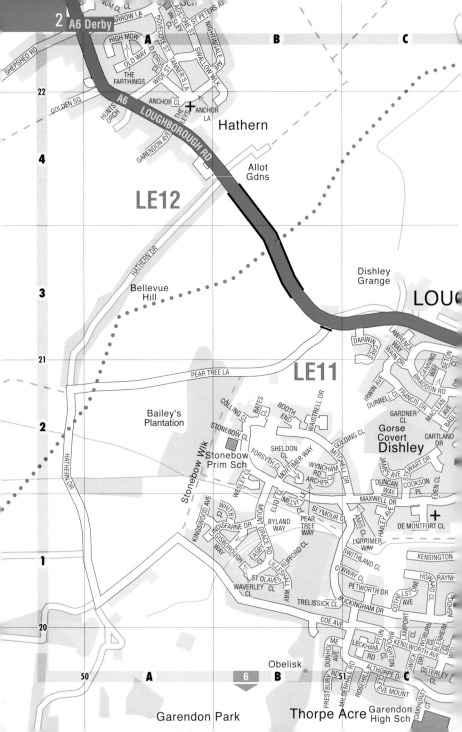

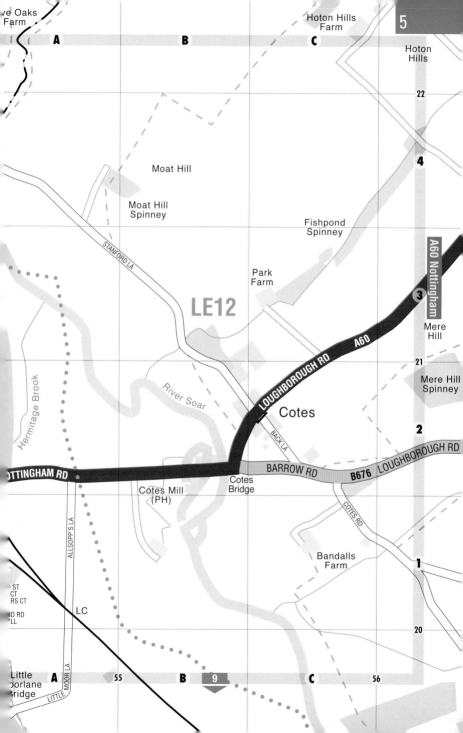

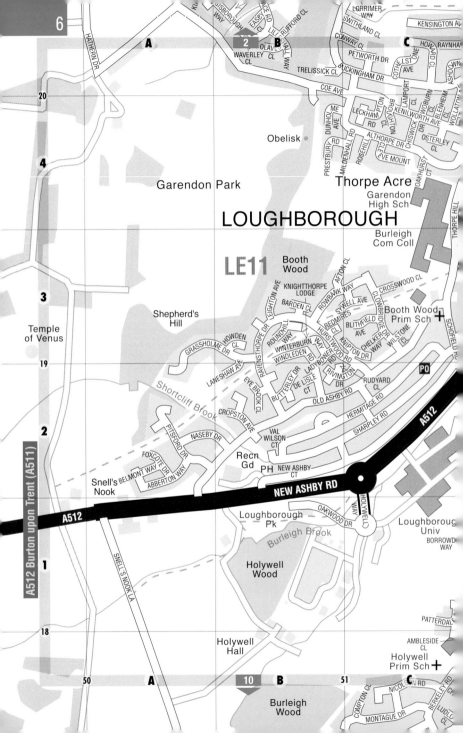

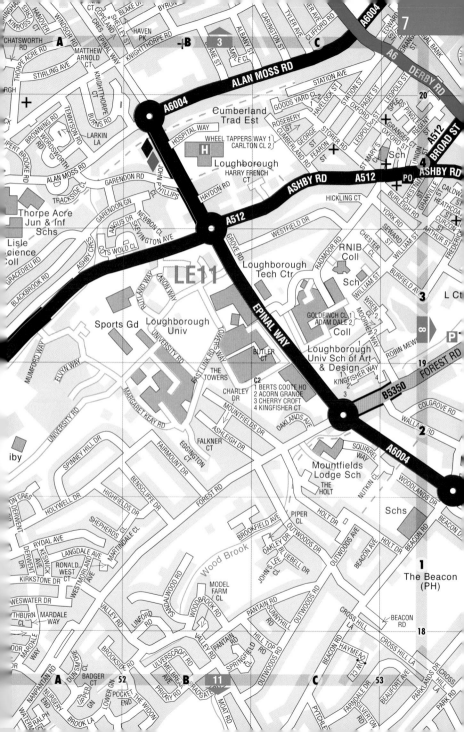

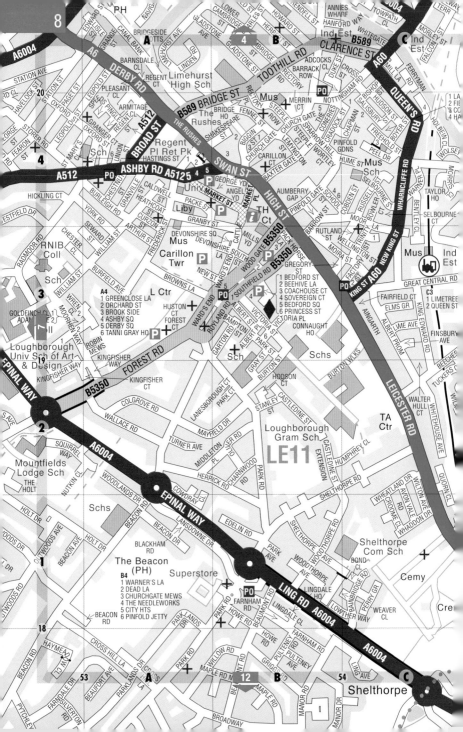

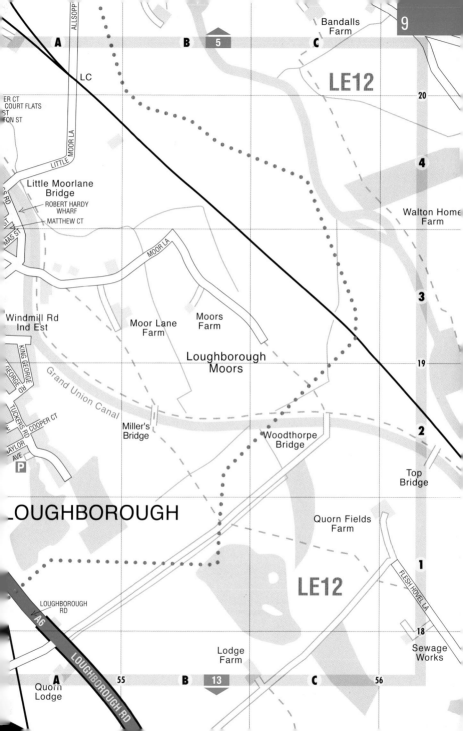

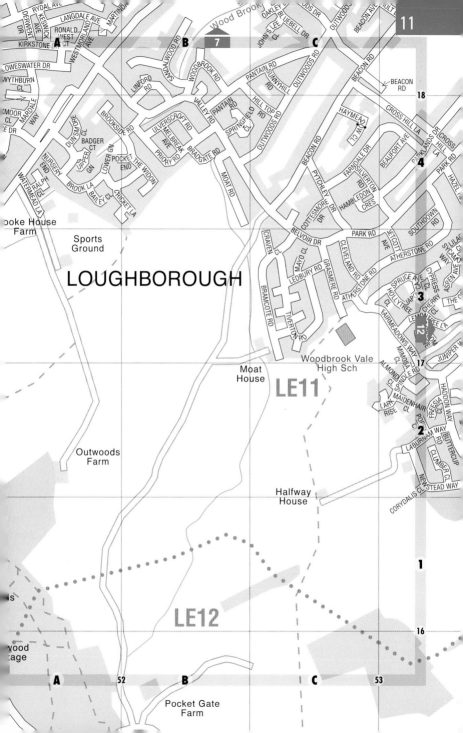

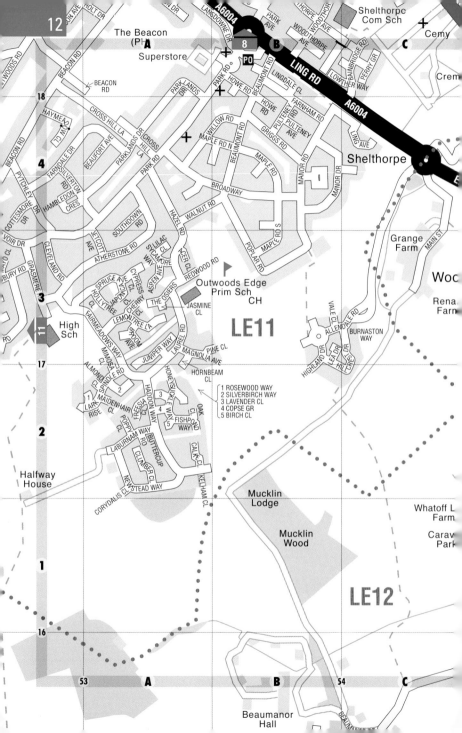

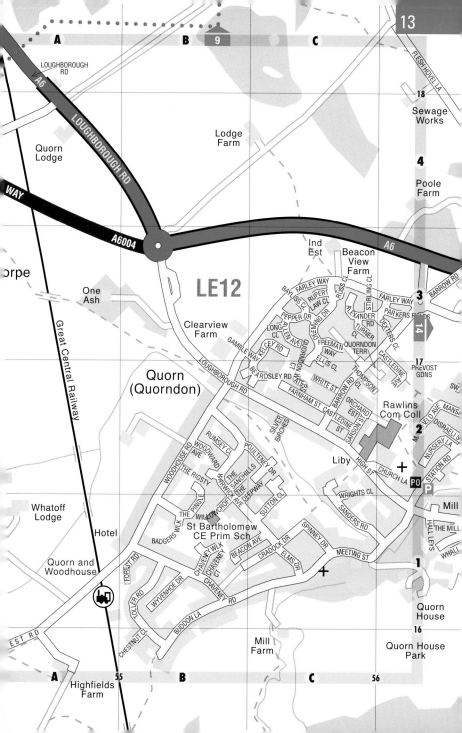

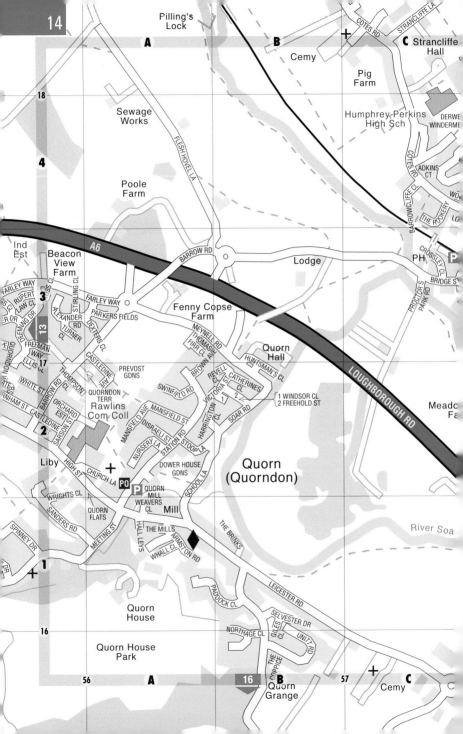

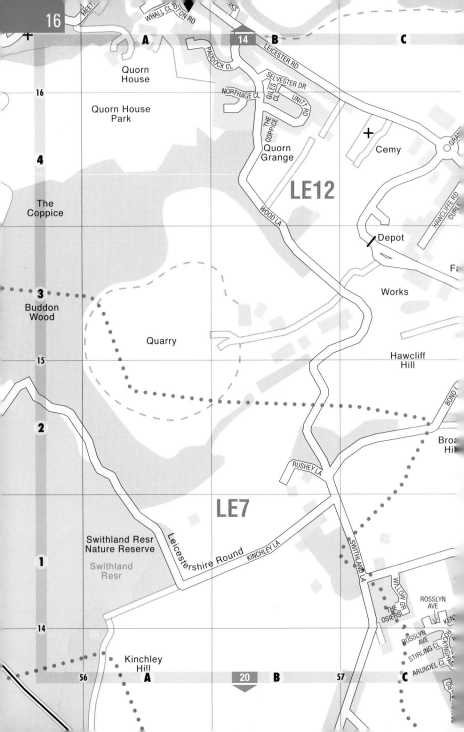

A   B   C

SILEBY RD

16

SLASH LA

4

BARROW RD

Sileby

WRIGHTS ACRE

HOMEFIELD RD
FOREST
BARRADALE AV
GREEN
HUDSON RISE
ST MARY'S RD
PARK RD

Redlands
Com Prim Sch

HIGHBRIDGE
KINGS ST
CHAPLIN CL
SWA

C3
1 OLD TANNERY DR
2 SIMONS WLK
3 LAWSON CL
4 WILLET CL
5 CYGNET CL
6 JORDEAN CT

HERRICK CL

LOVETT CT

3

PH

BRADGATE CL
BURTON CL
MOIR CL
HOBB
WIC

17

LITTLE CHURCH LA
HIGH ST
Sileby

BROOK
BACK LA
DUDLEY CT

ALBION RD
BANKS

15

MOUNTSORREL LA

LE12

THE MALTINGS

Liby

Works

MANOR DR

HARLEQUIN RD

MELODY DR

SAVILLE DR

KILBOURN

Weir

Leicestershire Round

River Soar

PRESTON CL

COSSINGTON RD

MILNER
FLAXLAND CRES
CL

2

LOUGHBOROUGH RD   A6

KINGFISHER RD

LYNTON CL
SHERRA

LARD RD

RUSH CL
CLOVER
ACRE
POTTLETS
MARL
FIELDS
ROW
FALLONG

QUAKER RD
WEST
ORCH
CHAL
ORCH
MIDDLE

LE7

LEICESTER RD
VERLIN CL

14

Garden
Centre

MAIN ST

Br
Fa

59   A   B   60   C

Cossington
CE Prim
Sch

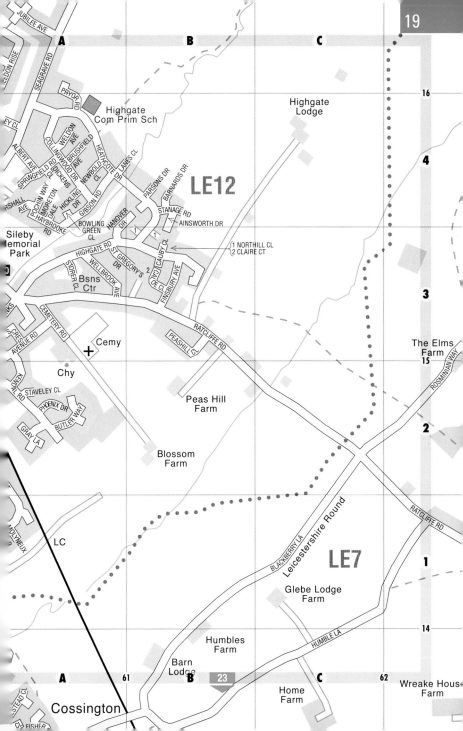

19

A B C

16

Highgate
Lodge

JUBILEE AVE

SELDON RISE

SEAGRAVE RD

PRYOR RD

EY CL

Highgate
Com Prim Sch

4

ALBERT AVE

WELDON
AVE

COLLINGWOOD RD

BRUSHFIELD
AVE

HEATHCOTE DR

NEWBOLD
CL

LANES CL

PARSONS DR

BARNARDS DR

LE12

SPRINGFIELD AVE

DICKENS

HICKLING
DR

GIBSON RD

P CHIN WAY

IMORETON
DALE

HANOVER
DR

STANAGE RD

AINSWORTH DR

RSHALL
AVE

HAYBROOKE
RD

BOWLING
GREEN
CL

1

1

1 NORTHILL CL
2 CLAIRE CT

Sileby
Memorial
Park

HIGHGATE RD

STORER CL

ST GREGORY'S
DR

WELLBROOK AVE

CAUBY CL

CACE CL

FINSBURY AVE

2

Bsns
Ctr

3

CEMETERY RD

PRESSLEY RD

AVENUE RD

Cemy

RATCLIFFE RD

PEASHILL C

The Elms
Farm

15

ROSMINIAN WAY

+

Chy

STAVELEY CL

KENT
AL RD

PHOENIX DR

BUTLER WAY

GRAY LA

Peas Hill
Farm

2

RATCLIFFE RD

Blossom
Farm

MOLYNEUX

LC

BLACKBERRY LA

Leicestershire Round

LE7

1

Glebe Lodge
Farm

14

HUMBLE LA

Humbles
Farm

Barn
Lodge

23

Home
Farm

Wreake House
Farm

A 61 B C 62

Cossington

STEAD CL

CL FISHER

61 62

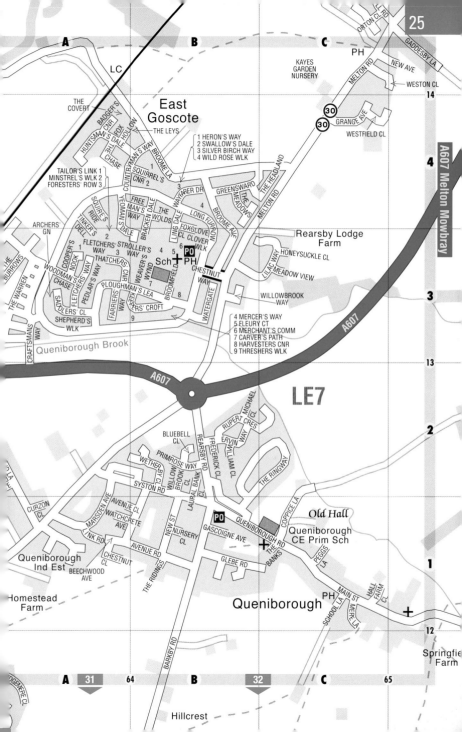

LC

THE COVERT

BADGER'S CNR

THE LEYS

East Goscote

HUNTSMAN'S DALE

FOX HOLLOW

THE CHASE

COUNTRYMAN'S WAY

BROOME LA

SQUIRREL'S CNR 2

WAYFARER DR

1 HERON'S WAY
2 SWALLOW'S DALE
3 SILVER BIRCH WAY
4 WILD ROSE WLK

TAILOR'S LINK 1
MINSTREL'S WLK 2
FORESTERS' ROW 3

FREE MAN'S WAY

YEOMAN'S DALE

BRACKEN DALE

THE WOLDS

LING DALE

LONG FURROW

FOXGLOVE CL CLOVER WLK

GREENSWARD

THE MEADOWS

BROOME AVE

THE HEADLAND

MELTON RD

Rearsby Lodge Farm

ARCHERS' GN

TINKER'S DELL

SQUIRE'S RIDE

FLETCHERS' STROLLER'S WAY WAY

COOPER'S NOOK

PEDLARS WAY

THATCHERS CNR

WEAVER'S WYND

BROOMFIELD

Sch

PO PH

CHESTNUT WAY

HONEYSUCKLE CL

LILAC WAY

MEADOW VIEW

THE BURROWS

THE WARREN

WOODMAN'S CHASE

SADDLERS' CL

FLETCHERS CL

SHEPHERD'S WLK

PLOUGHMAN'S LEA

FARRIERS WAY

REAPERS' CROFT

WATERGATE

WILLOWBROOK WAY

CRAFTSMANS WAY

Queniborough Brook

4 MERCER'S WAY
5 FLEURY CT
6 MERCHANT'S COMM
7 CARVER'S PATH
8 HARVESTERS CNR
9 THRESHERS WLK

A607

LE7

KAYES GARDEN NURSERY

PH

MELTON RD

ORTON RD

GADDESBY LA

NEW AVE

WESTON CL

14

30

30

GRANGE AVE

WESTFIELD CL

4

A607 Melton Mowbray

3

A607

13

BLUEBELL CL

RUPERT CL

MICHAEL CL

ERVIN WAY

WILLIAM CL

FREDERICK RD

PRIMROSE WAY

WETHERBY CL

WILLOW BROOK CL

SYSTON RD

REARSBY RD

LAURAL BANK

THE RINGWAY

COPPICE LA

2

Old Hall

CURZON CL

MARSDEN AVE

AVENUE CL

WATCHCRETE AVE

LINK RD

NEW ST

NURSERY CL

AVENUE RD

CHESTNUT

THE RIDINGS

GASCOIGNE AVE

PO

QUENIBOROUGH RD

GLEBE RD

THE BANKS

PEGGS LA

Queniborough CE Prim Sch

Queniborough Ind Est

BEECHWOOD AVE

Homestead Farm

BARKBY RD

Queniborough

PH

SCHOOL LA

MAIN ST

MERIL LA

HALL FARM CL

1

12

Springfield Farm

NGENERE CL

Hillcrest

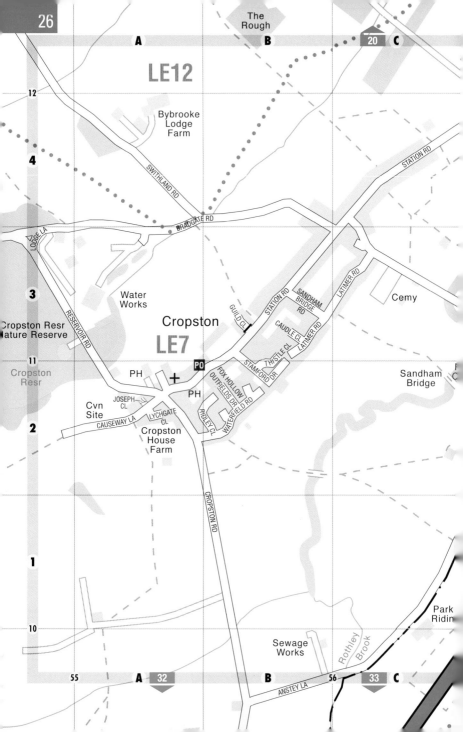

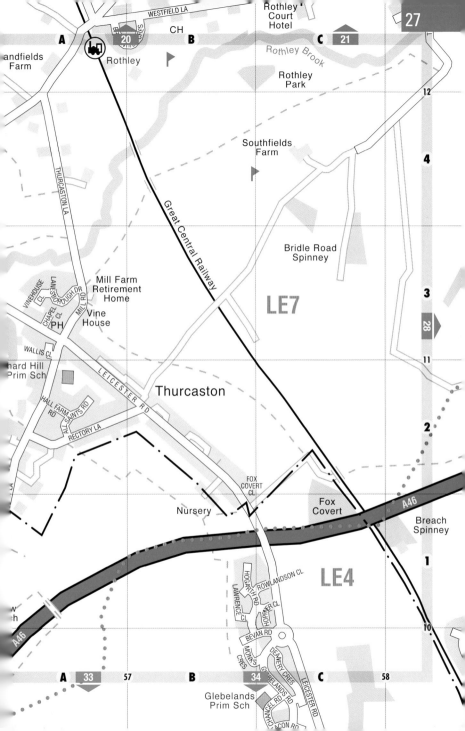

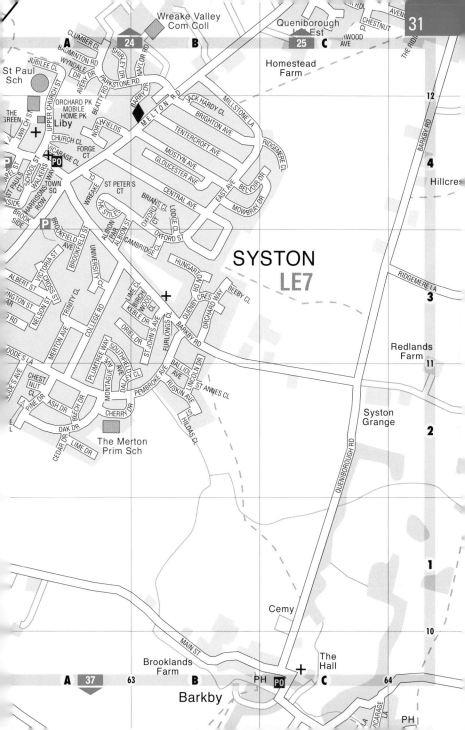

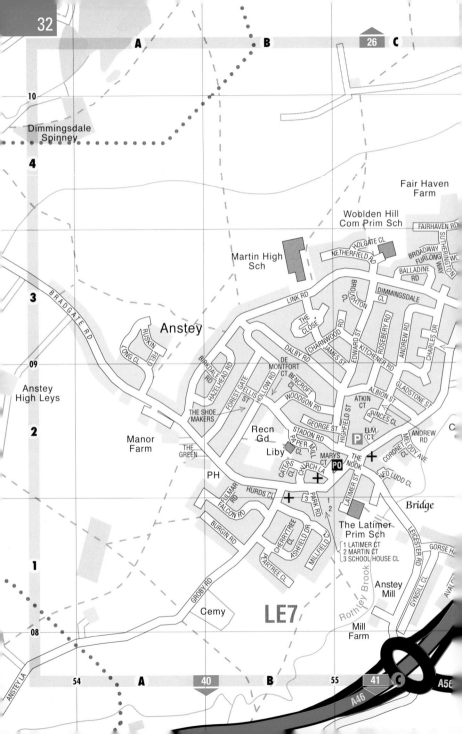

A   B   26   C

10

Dimmingsdale
Spinney

4

Fair Haven
Farm

Wooblen Hill
Com Prim Sch

FAIRHAVEN RD

Martin High
Sch

HOLGATE CL

NETHERFIELD RD

BROADWAY

SUTHERINGTON

FURLONG WAY

BALLADINE
RD

BROUGHTON

LINK RD

THE
CLOSE

CHARNWOOD RD

BROOKS RD

EDWARD ST

KITCHENER RD

ROSEBERY RD

ANDREW RD

CHARLES DR

DIMMINGSDALE
CL

3

BRADGATE RD

Anstey

RUSKIN FIELD

LONG CL

DALBY RD

JAMES ST

09

Anstey
High Leys

BIRKDALE RD

HAZELHEAD RD

DE
MONTFORT
CT

BENCROFT
CL

HOLLOW RD

WOODGON RD

HIGHFIELD ST

ALBION ST

GLADSTONE ST

ATKIN
CT

PRINCES CL

FOREST GATE

GELLIS ST

ANDREW
RD

C

THE SHOE
MAKERS

GEORGE ST

ELM
CT

CORONET CL

MELODY AVE

2

Manor
Farm

THE
GREEN

Recn
Gd

STADON RD

PAPER
MILL
CL

P

THE
NOOK

Liby

MARYS
CT

PO

PH

CATERS CL

CHURCH LA

NED LUDD CL

Bridge

HURDS CL

PARK RD

LATIMER ST

LEICESTER RD

GORSE H

FULMAR RD

FALCON RD

3

1

The Latimer
Prim Sch

1

BURGIN RD

CHERRYTREE
CL

ASHFIELD DR

MILLFIELD

2

1 LATIMER CT
2 MARTIN CT
3 SCHOOL HOUSE CL

GYNSILL CL

AVAL

PEARTREE CL

Anstey
Mill

GROBY RD

Cemy

LE7

Rothley Brook

Mill
Farm

08

ANSTEY LA

54   A   40   B   55   41   C   A56

A46

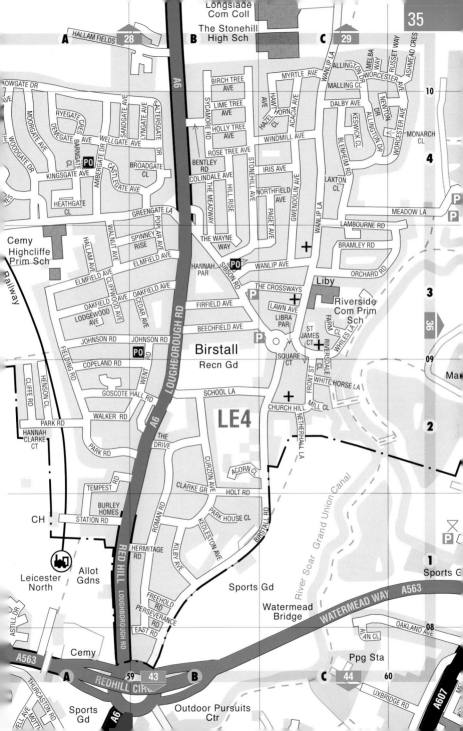

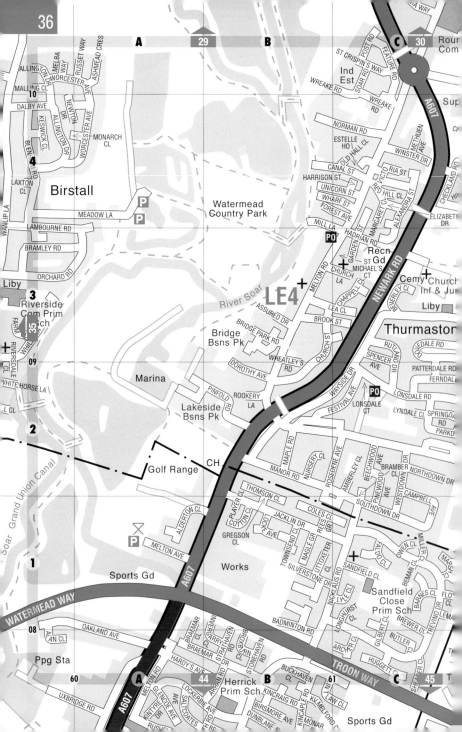

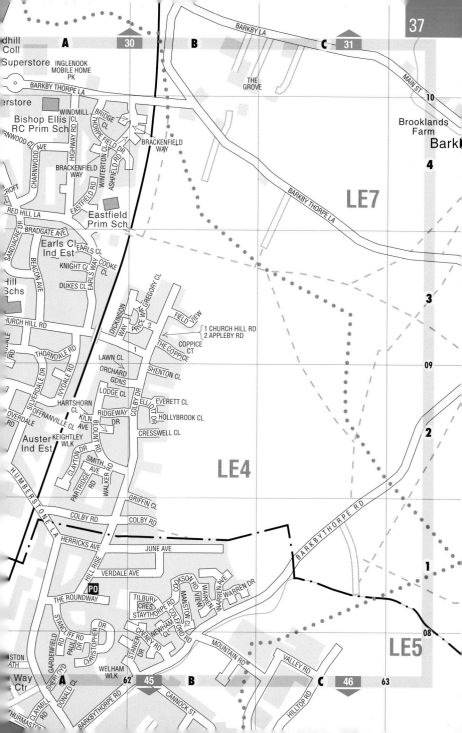

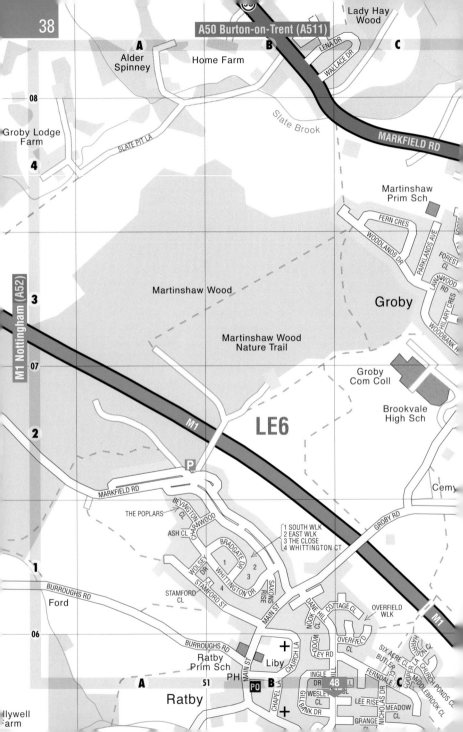

A **B** **C**

A50 Burton-on-Trent (A511)

Lady Hay Wood

LENA DR

WALLACE DR

Alder Spinney

Home Farm

08

Slate Brook

MARKFIELD RD

Groby Lodge Farm

SLATE PIT LA

4

Martinshaw Prim Sch

FERN CRES

WOODLANDS DR

PARKLANDS AVE

FOREST CL

LAWNWOOD RD

HILARY CRES

WOODBANK H

Martinshaw Wood

Groby

3

Martinshaw Wood Nature Trail

07

Groby Com Coll

M1

Brookvale High Sch

2

LE6

Cemy

P

MARKFIELD RD

THE POPLARS

BEVINGTON CL

CHARNWOOD

ASH CL

BRADGATE DR

GROBY RD

1 SOUTH WLK
2 EAST WLK
3 THE CLOSE
4 WHITTINGTON CT

M1 Nottingham (A52)

M1

1

BURROUGHS RD

WOLSEY DR

WHITTINGTON DR

STAMFORD ST

SAXONS RISE

MAIN ST

DANE HILL

COTTAGE CL

OVERFIELD WLK

Ford

STAMFORD CL

NOOK CL

BLOOM LEY RD

OVERFIELD CL

SIX ACRE CL

HARRISON CL

CHURCH PONDS CL

MIDDLEBROOK CL

BUTLER CL

06

BURROUGHS RD

Ratby Prim Sch

PH

Liby

CHURCH LA

INGLE DR

WESLEY CL

FERNDALE CL

NICHOLAS CL

MEADOW CL

COOPER LA

A 51 **B** 48 **C**

MAIN ST

CHAPEL LA

PO

GILLITT CL

BANK DR

LEE RISE

GRANGE

llywell Farm

Ratby

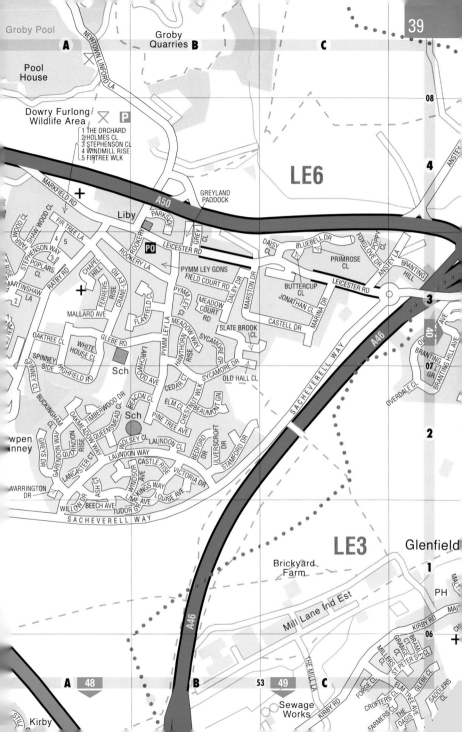

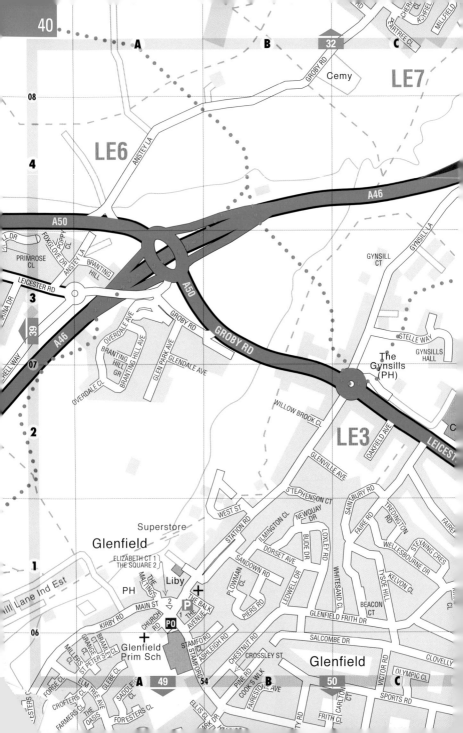

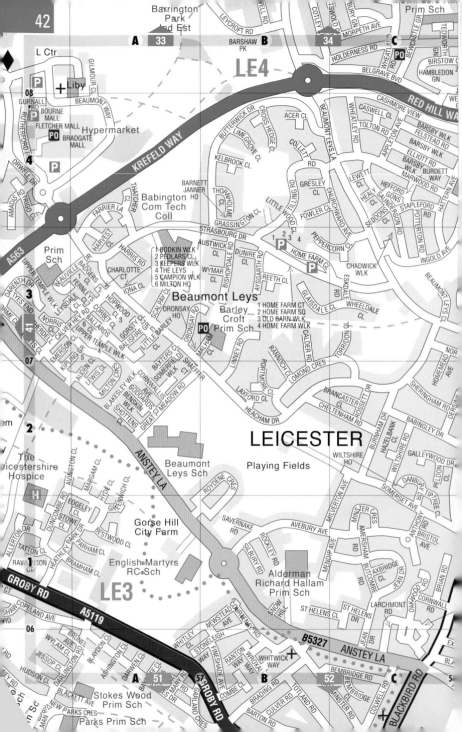

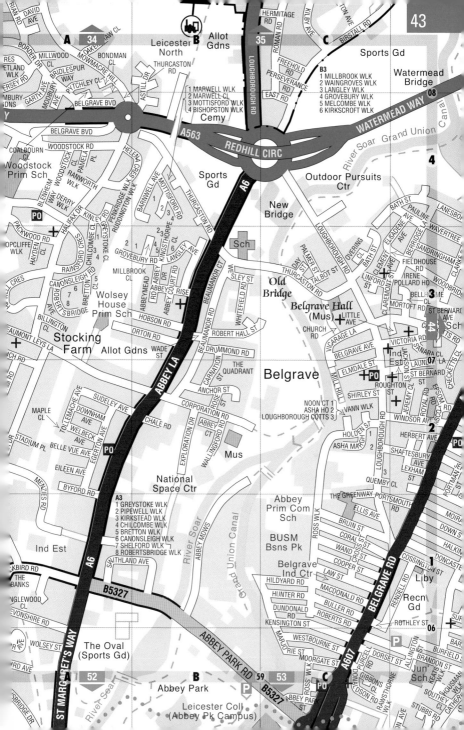

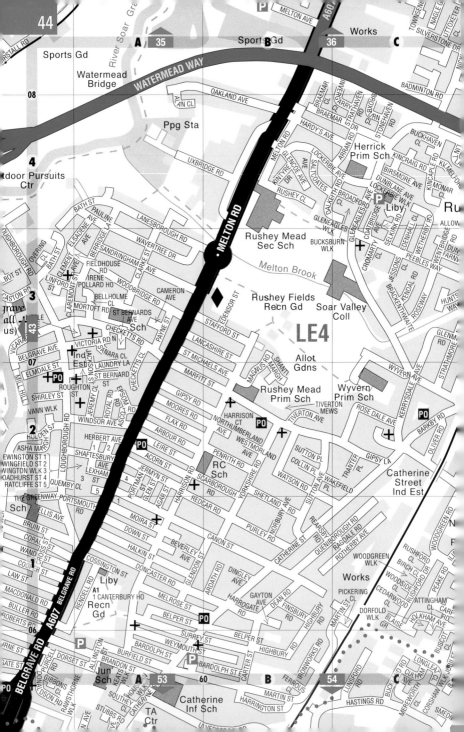

LE4

A 37 B C

WARREN DR
WARREN AVE
BARKBYTHORPE RD
WARREN RD/VIEW

08

MOUNTAIN RD

VALLEY RD

HILLTOP RD

4

Hamilton Bsns Pk

CANNOCK ST

WATERSIDE RD

B3
1 LAKEVIEW CT
2 CRANELEY CT
3 BELGRAVE CT
4 GRANBY CT
5 BLACKSMITH PL

Hamilton

GLENCOTE RD
SHIPTON
DALTON RD
HERITAGE WAY

TUXFORD RD

Hope Hamilton
CE Prim Sch

BROMPTON RD
BIRKBY CL
HORNBY RD

HAMILTON CIRC
PICKHILL RD

HIGHCLIFFE RD

SANDHILLS AVE

LAKEVIEW CHASE

SADDLER RD
CARTY RD
HILLIER

SUNDIAL RD
CARRINGTON RD

RICHMORE RD

MAIDENHEAD AVE

BAKERS WAY

THE MALTINGS

P

3

45

63

Humberstone Farm

SPEEDWELL DR

COLUMBINE RD

CRANSLEY CL
EYEBROOK
CLOVERDALE RD

TRILLIUM

SHEPHERD CT
WAINWRIGHT AVE

MASON ROW

HERITAGE WAY

P

A6030

07

SANDHILLS AVE

BELLFLOWER RD
JASMINE CL
EDGEFIELD
LARKSPUR CL
ORPINE RD

MALLOW
HAREBELL CL

OAKBRIDGE
OAKDALE

ELMIN
STONECROP RD
WINTERGREEN
CELANDINE RD

GAMEKEEPERS CT

HAMILTON CT

ORCHID

SAMPHIRE
CL

BRYONY RD

2

Quakesick Spinney

CAWSTON CL
SAXTHORPE RD
BINTREE CL

ANTRINGHAM

HOLLY BANK

COLTSFOOT

COLUMBINE RD

RAMSON CL

SUNDEW RD

CHARLOCK RD

BURDOCK

MARSHAM CL

HANWORTH CL

GUESTWICK GN
ELMTREE CL

KESTREL LA

BESSINGHAM
WILLOWTREE

HONEYSUCKLE
GOLDCROFT TREFOIL CL

ASHTREE RD

FOXGLOVE RD

BRAMBLE CL
HAZELDENE RD

SORREL RD

LE5

ATTLEBRIDGE

MAIDENWELL AVE
BURNET

MEADOWSWEET

Kestrels' Field Prim Sch

Keyham Lodge Sch

Liby

YARROW CL
CRANESBILL

KEYHAM LA

Manor Farm

THURMASTON LA

Church Farm House

HAMILTON WAY

A563

Preston Rise

FERN RISE

CHESTNUT

BARRY RD

SELBY AVE
CRAYFORD WAY
NEWLYN PAR
LIMEHURST RD

GREENBANK RD

Humberstone
Jun & Inf Schs

COLIN GRUNDY DR

KEYHAM LA

Humberstone Garden

KEYHAM LA

LABURNUM RD
LILAC AVE

ROSEBARN AVE
AUSTIN RISE

NETHERHALL RD

Nether Hall Sch

1

Humberstone Manor

LOWER KEYHAM LA

HANOVER CL
HUMBER CL

KEYHAM CL

Liby

HUNGARTON BLVD

NETHERHALL RD
MOAT

TOLCARNE RD
WINSLOW GN

Scraptoft Valley Prim Sch

06

WARREN CL
LUDSTER CL
HOUSE GDNS

MANOR DR

STEINS LA
HESILRIGE WLK
HOTOFT RD

ARNCLIFFE RD

GRANTHAM RD
UPPER
ARMADALE GN

MOORFIELDS

ARMADALE DR

KEYHAM CEDAR CT

STANLEY DR
LOBBS WOOD CL
VICARAGE RD

MAIN ST

ABBOTS CL
COTS CL

P

A

55

63

A563

WANSBECK GDNS
ST MARYS AV
ST MARYS

B

WIGLEY RD

UPPER HALL CL

56

St Joseph's RC Prim Sch

C

LYMINGTON RD
LYNMOUTH RD

Recn Gd

Barkby Thorpe
Spinney

A   B   C

08

4

LE7

3

07

Hamilton
Grounds

Lodge
Farm

2

CH

Hamilton
Com Coll

Hall
Farm

KEYHAM LA W

HAMILTON LA

SEATON RISE

MAPLIN RD

Hamilford CL

PORTCULLIS RD

Nether Hall

1 BARONET WAY
2 RAYLEIGH WAY
3 RAMSEY WAY
4 RAMSEY GDNS

CHURCH CRES

RAYLEIGH GN

Barkford CL

2

BRIARFIELD DR

3   4

ARCHWAY RD

RINGWOOD RD

BRINDLEY RISE

NEW   ROMNEY CRES

1

06

Sports Gd

NEW ROMNEY CRES

FLATHOLME RD

HAMILTON LA

HALL RD

THE DRIVE

HINKS AVE

KEATS WAY

THE MOUNT

BEEBY RD

MARLSBURY A

The
Mount

ELSTREE AVE

BANKSIDE

NEW ROMNEY CL

A   56

PO

B   65   57   C

COVERT LA

MAIN ST

COULTER CL

MITCHELL GR

Scraptoft

CROFT RISE

STOCKS RD

CHURCH

BEEBY RD

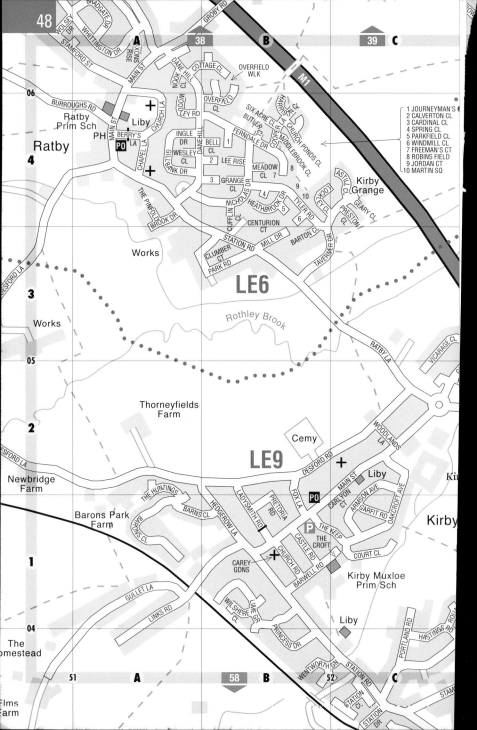

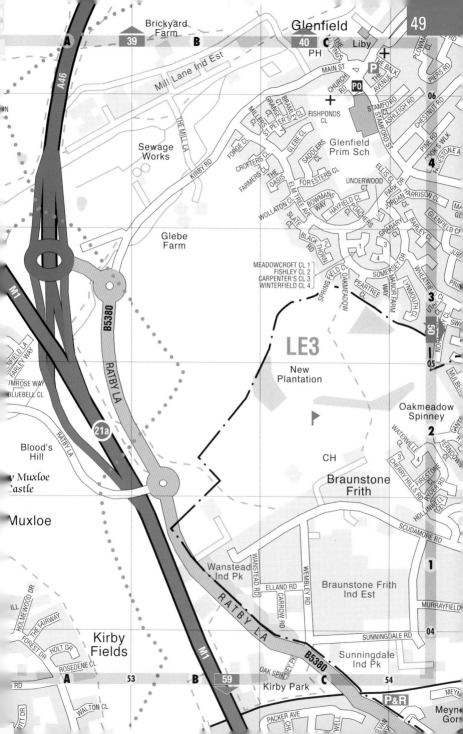

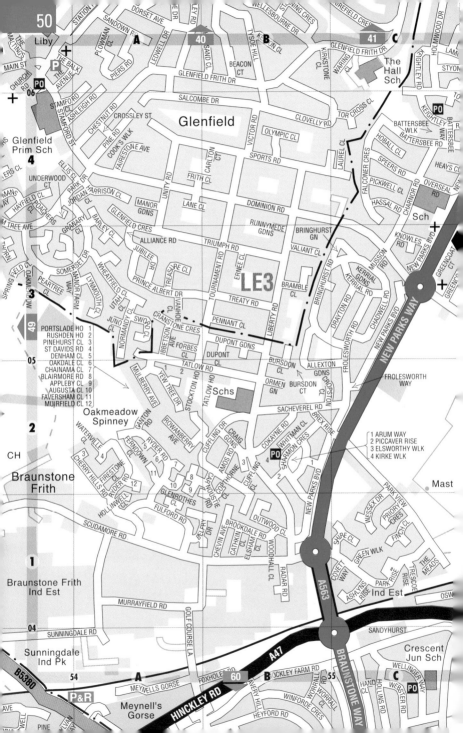

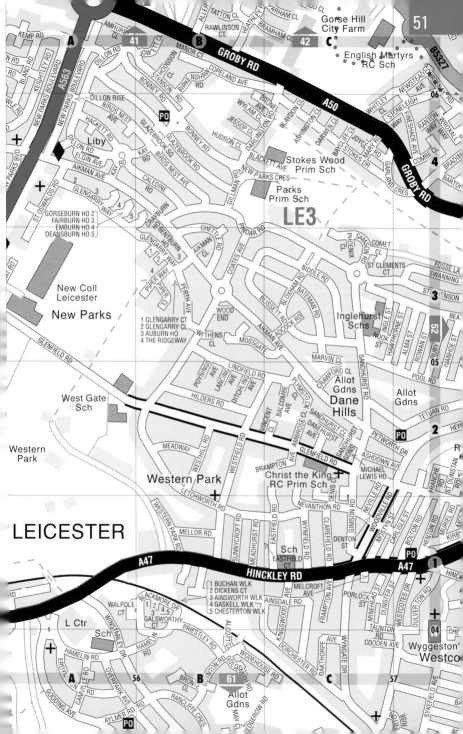

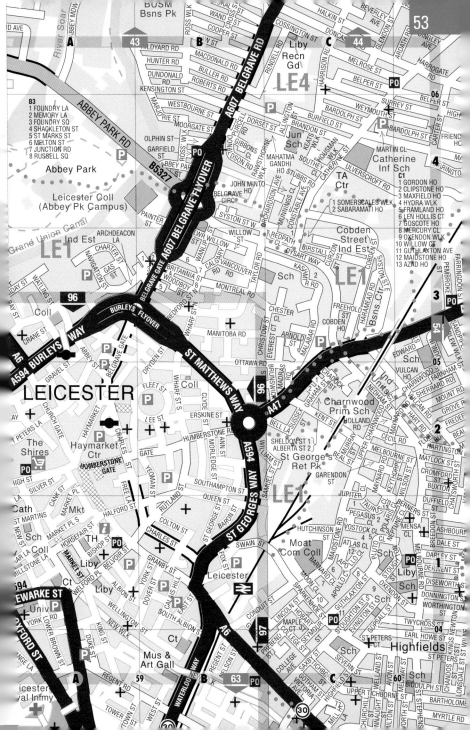

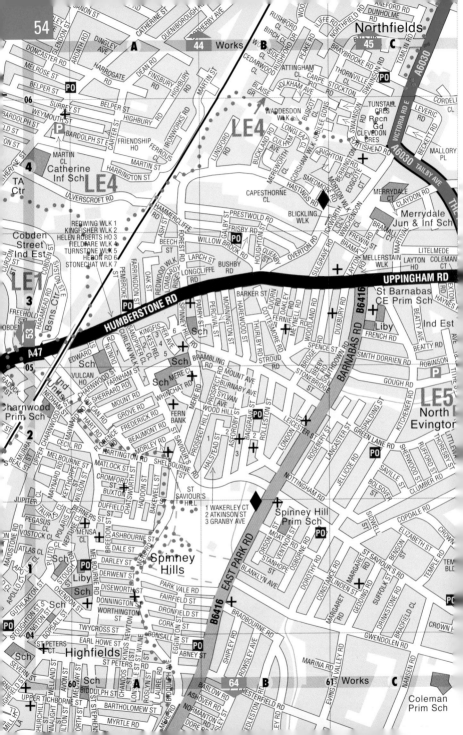

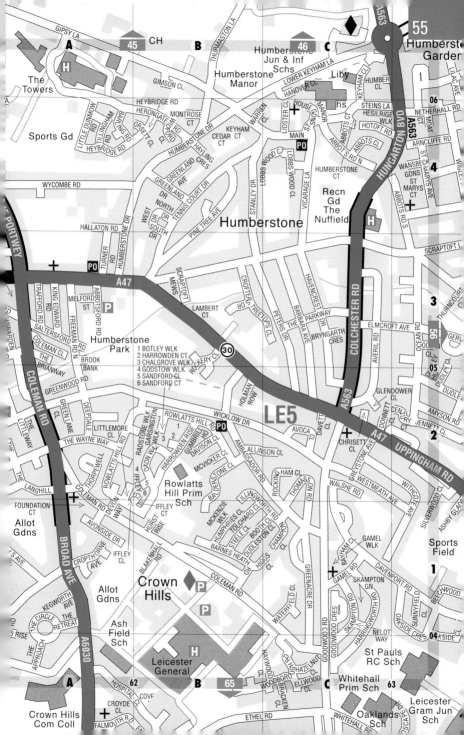

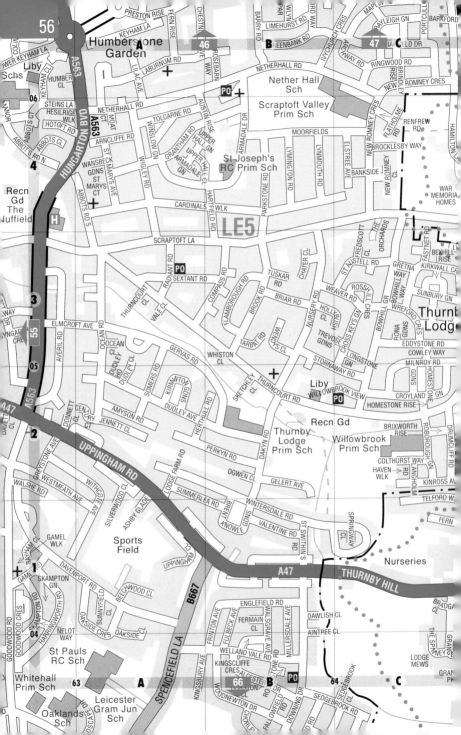

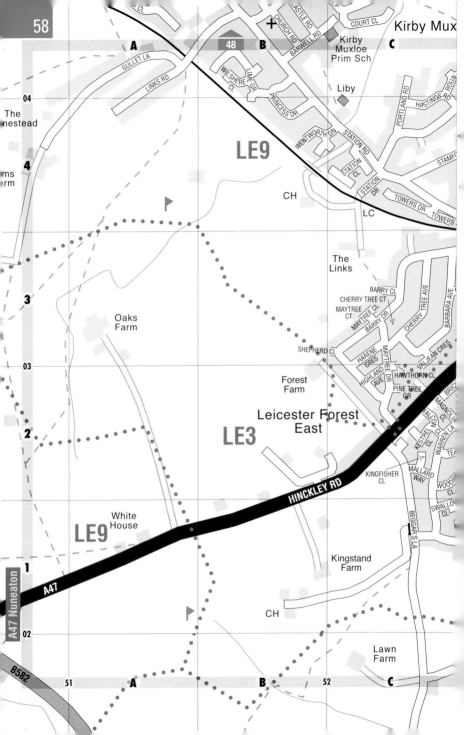

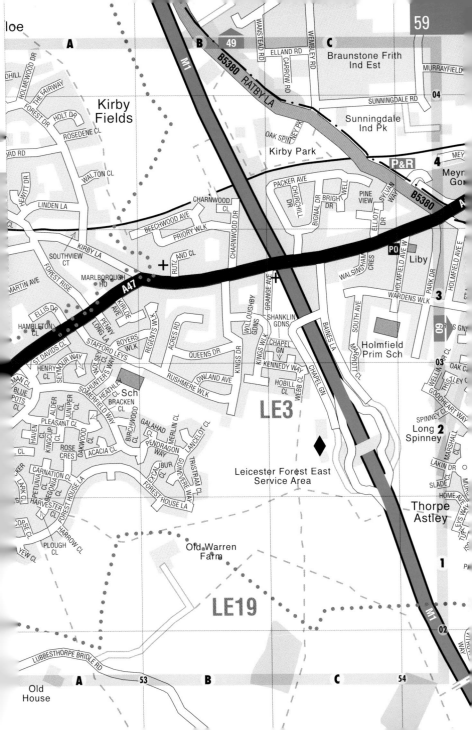

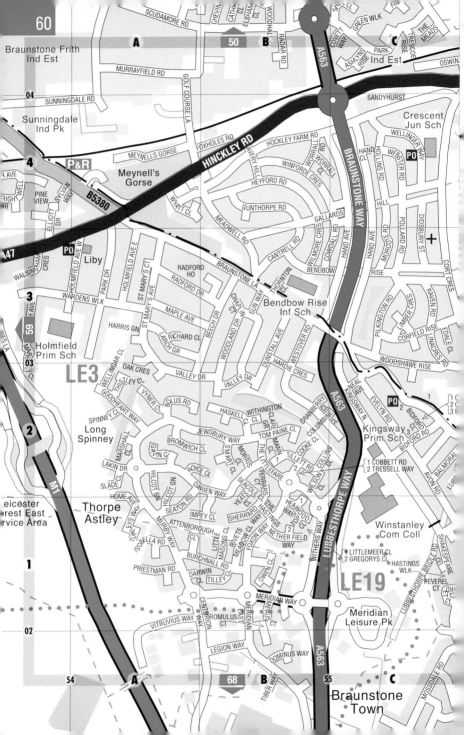

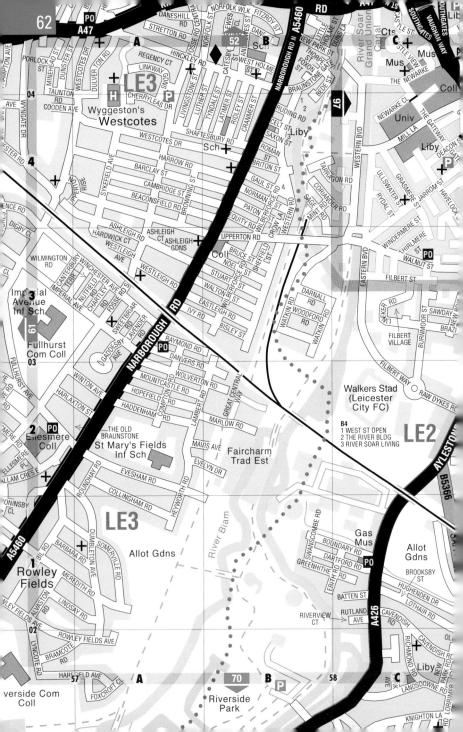

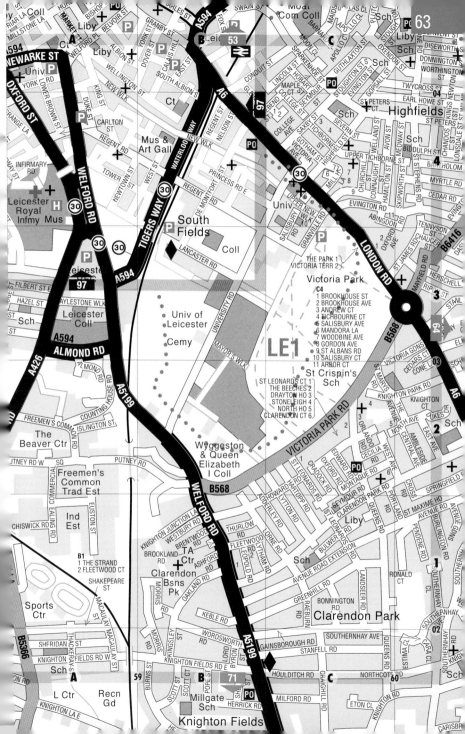

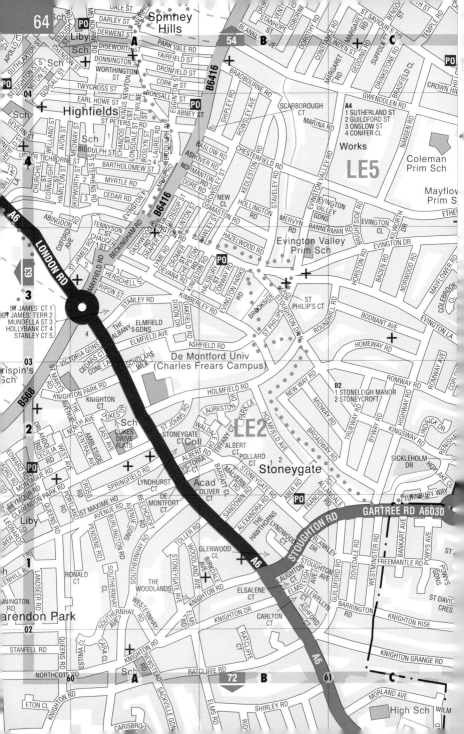

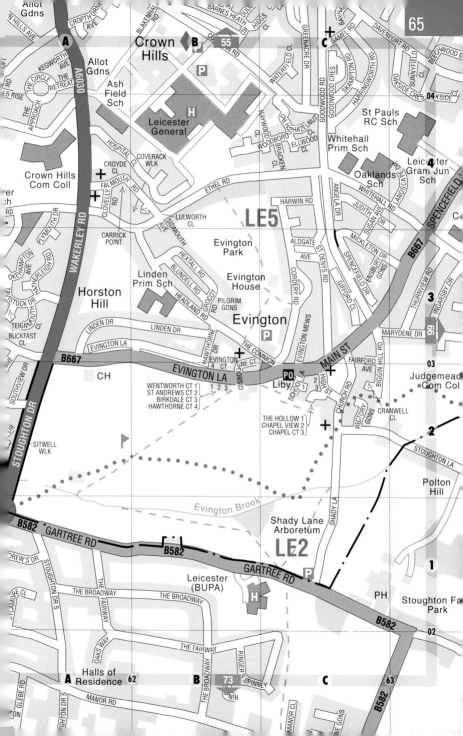

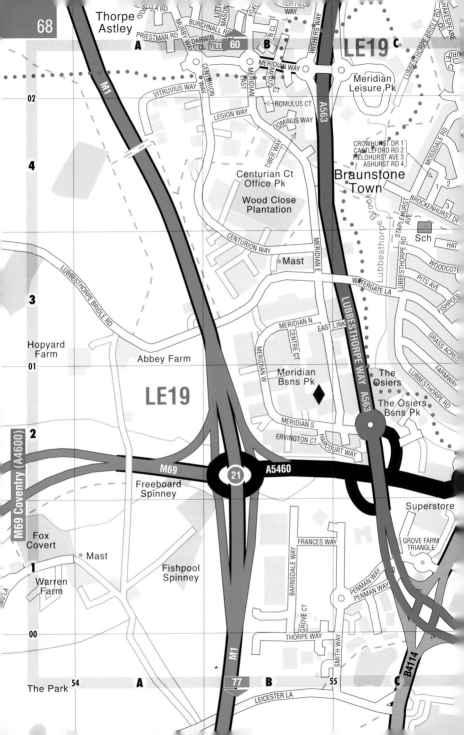

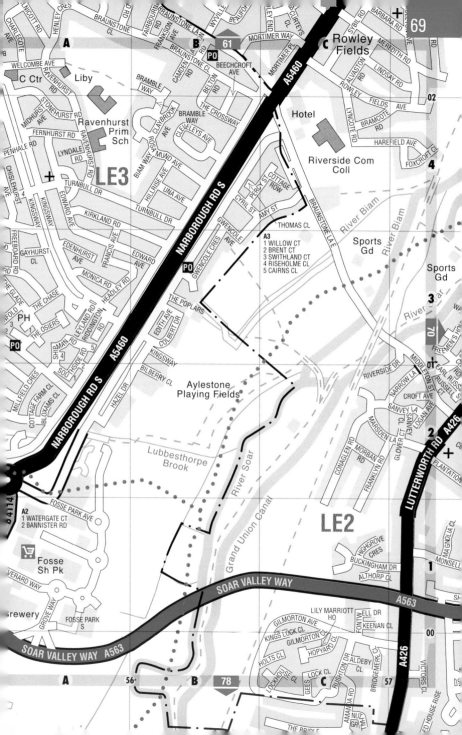

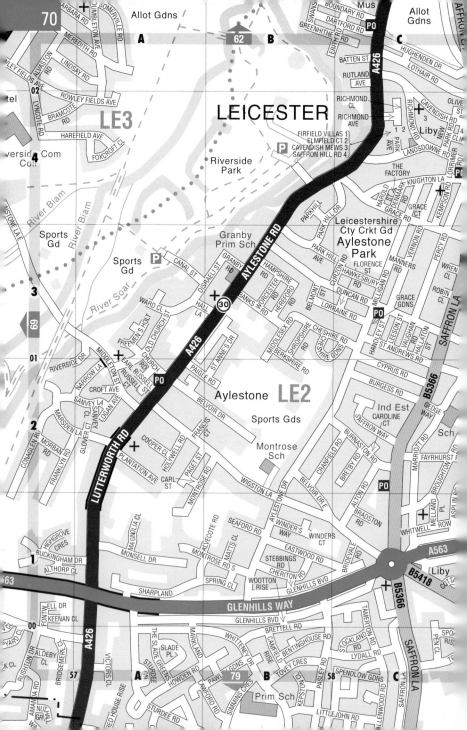

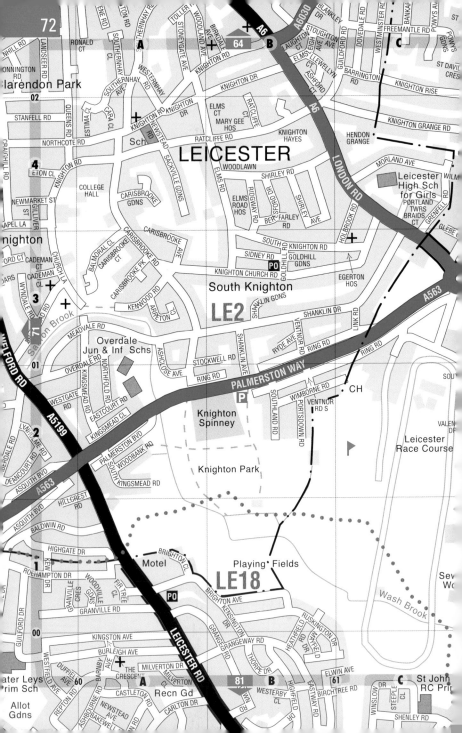

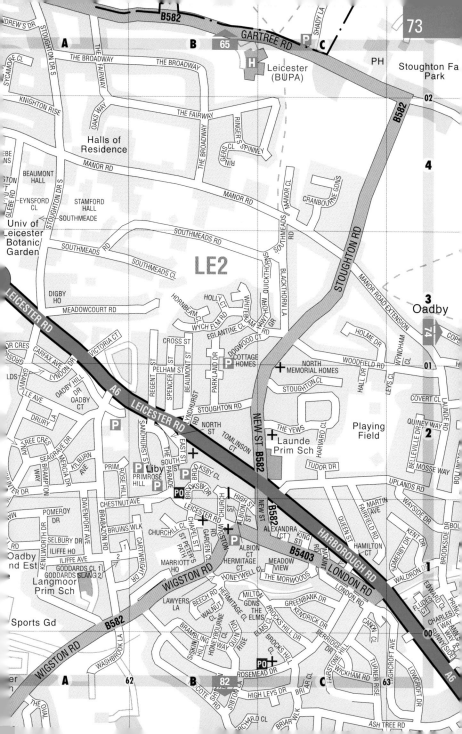

HOUGHTON LA

HOUGHTON LA

A

B

67

C

Clarke's
Bush

02

GAULBY LA

4

Leicester
Airport

3

01

LE2

Mast

Mast

2

MERE RD

Great Stretton

+

GARTREE RD

Oadby Lodge
Farm

1

00

LE8

A

65

THE SPINNEY

B

CHESTNUT DR

C

66

THE AVENUE

The
Wilderness

Stretton
Hall

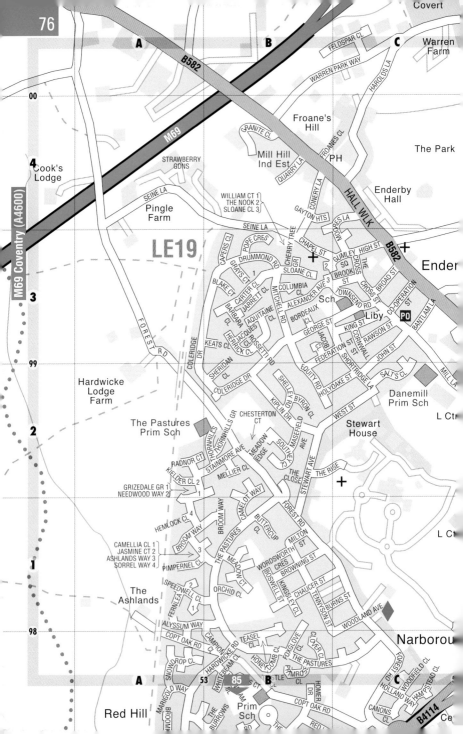

Covert

Warren Farm

B582

WARREN PARK WAY

FELDSPAR CL

HAROLDS LA

C

B

A

M69

Cook's Lodge

STRAWBERRY GDNS

GRANITE CL

Froane's Hill

FROANES CL

QUARRY LA

CONERLY LA

PH

The Park

Enderby Hall

HALL WLK

SEINE LA

Pingle Farm

WILLIAM CT 1
THE NOOK 2
SLOANE CL 3

SEINE LA

MOSES LA

GAYTON HTS

GUMLEY SQ

HIGH ST

B582

+

Ender

LE19

CAPERS CL

POPE CRES

CHERRY TREE

GR

CHAPEL ST

THE CROSS

BROAD ST

BROOK

CO-OPERATION ST

GRAYS CL

DRUMMOND RD

1

SLOANE CL

COLUMBIA CL

ALEXANDER AVE 3

Sch

TOWNSEND RD

BANTLAM LA

Liby

P0

BLAKE CT

CARTER CL

JARRETT CL

MITCHEL RD

BORDEAUX CL

GEORGE ST

KING ST

RAWSON ST

JOHN ST

MILL LA

FOREST RD

BARBARA CL

AQUITAINE CL

JACQUES

JACOB ST

CORNWALL

COLERIDGE DR

KEATS CL

HERRICK CL

ROSSETTI RD

FEDERATION ST

SHORTRIDGE

SALT'S CL

SHERIDAN CL

RAWSON

Danemill Prim Sch

L Ctr

Hardwicke Lodge Farm

COLERIDGE DR

SHELLEY RD

BYRON CL

EQUITY RD

HOLYOAKE ST

WEST ST

L C

The Pastures Prim Sch

THORNHILLS GR

CHESTERTON CT

KIPLIN DR

MASEFIELD

Stewart House

RADNOR CT

THORNHILLS GR

STAINMORE AVE

MEADOW EDGE

SOUTHEY

STEWART AVE

THE RISE

+

KIELDER CL 2

MELLIER CL

THE CLOSE

GRIZEDALE GR 1
NEEDWOOD WAY 2

1

CAMELOT WAY

FOREST RD

HEMLOCK CL 4

BROOM WAY

BUTTERCUP CL

MILTON ST

L C

CAMELLIA CL 1
JASMINE CT 2
ASHLANDS WAY 3
SORREL WAY 4

BROOM WAY

THE PASTURES

WORDSWORTH CRES

BROWNING ST

3

PIMPERNEL CL

MEADOW CT

ORCHID CL

BOSWELL ST

KINGSLEY CL

CHAUCER ST

FENNYSON ST

BURNS ST

The Ashlands

SPEEDWELL CL

2

FERNLEA

1

ALYSSUM WAY

WOODLAND AVE

Narborou

SNOWDROP CL

COPT OAK RD

CAMPION

HARDWICKE RD

WHITEBEAM RD

TEASEL CL

HONEYCOMB CL

FOXGLOVE

CLOVER CL

THE PASTURES

PR MRO

HOMER DR

FOREST CL

WOODFIELD CL

HOLLAND WAY

HAMPSTEAD CL

Red Hill

MARIGOLD WAY

BROOM

THE BURROWS

Prim Sch

STLE

COPT OAK RD

CANONS CL

B4114

Ce

53

85

B

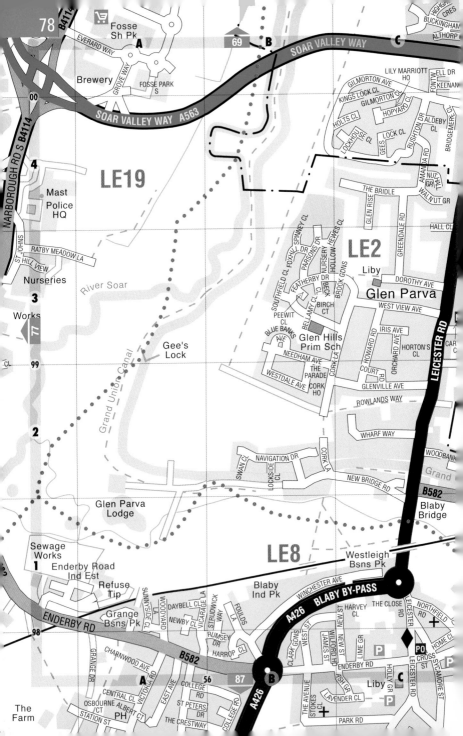

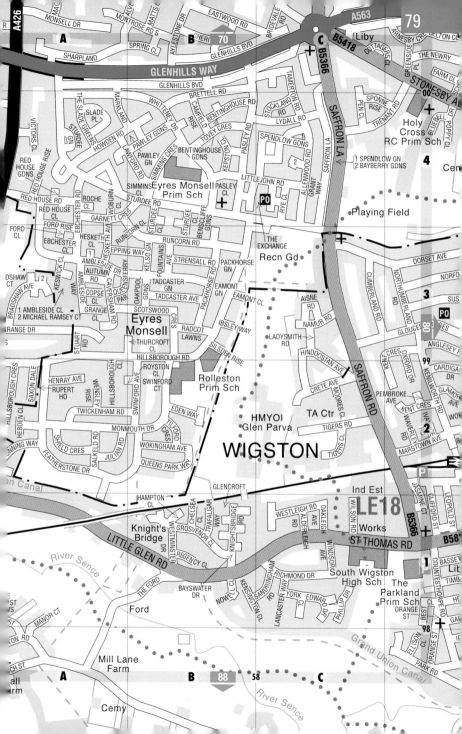

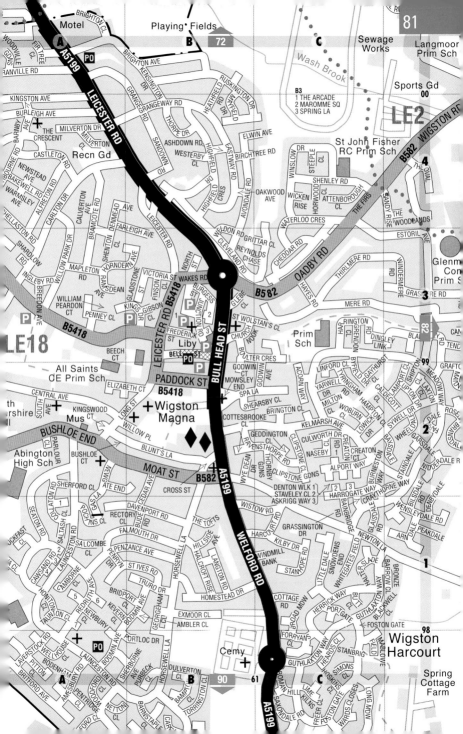

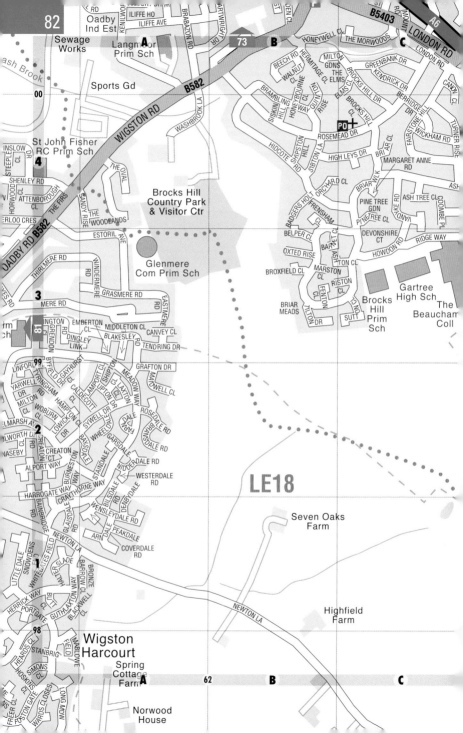

Oadby
Ind Est

Sewage
Works

ILIFFE HO
ILIFFE AVE

Langmoor
Prim Sch

A

73

B

HONEYWELL CL

THE MORWOODS

C

B5403

LONDON RD

Sports Gd

WIGSTON RD

B582

WASHBROOK LA

BEECH RD
WALNUT

HERMITAGE CL

MILTON
GDNS
THE
ELMS

GREENBANK DR

LONDON RD

BRAMBLING

HILL

HOMEBOURNE
WAY

QUIN CL

BROCKS
HILL
CL

KENDRICK DR

BROCKS HILL DR

BERRIDGE

FAIRSTONE
HILL

WICKHAM RD

CANDY CL

TURNER RISE

00

St John Fisher
RC Prim Sch

WIGSTON RD

PO

ROSEMEAD DR

SHIPSTON
HILL

SIBTON LA

AR CL

HIGH LEYS DR

BRI

MARGARET ANNE
RD

ASH TREE CL

COOMBE PL

ASH

INSLOW
CL

STEEPLE
CL

4

SHENLEY RD

ATTENBOROUGH
CL

HORWOOD

THE FIRS

SANDY RISE

THE OVAL

THE
WOODLANDS

THE

Brocks Hill
Country Park
& Visitor Ctr

HIDCOTE

ORCHARD CL

BADGERS HOLT

FRENSHAM
CL

BRIAR
WLK

PINE TREE
GDN

PINE TREE CL

VANDY KE RD

DEVONSHIRE
CT

HOWDON RD

RIDGE WAY

ERLOO CRES

B582

OADBY RD

ESTORIL AVE

THIRLMERE RD

WINDERMERE
RD

Glenmere
Com Prim Sch

BELPER CL

OXTED RISE

BROXFIELD CL

BARNET

MARSTON
CL

FENTON
CL

RISTON
CL

Brocks
Hill
Prim
Sch

Gartree
High Sch

The
Beauchamp
Coll

3

MERE RD

GRASMERE RD

EASTMERE
RD

EMBERTON
CL

MIDDLETON CL

BLAKESLEY RD

CANVEY CL

TENDRING DR

BRIAR
MEADS

MILTON
DR

SUTT

81

GRENDON
RD

DINGLEY
LINK

GRAFTON DR

99

LINFORT

BYFIELD

GAYHURST

CALDECOTT

SHIPTON

UPTON CL

LAXTON

MEADOW WAY

MAXWELL CL

YARWELL
DR

TRINGHAM CL

HAMPTON CL

LAMPORT CL

SYWELL DR

ROSEDALE RD

MILTON
CL

WOBURN
DR

LOWICK DR

BASSDALE

WHEELDALE

FARN
DALE

BRA

BRISDALE
RD

2

ELMARSH AV

WASEBY

CREATION
CT

ALPORT WAY

SYWELL DR

STANDALE

NIDDALE

DALE RD

WESTERDALE
RD

HARROGATE WAY

BURNSTON

CRAYTHORNE WAY

GLAISDALE

BILSDALE

DENBYDALE

LE18

BAINBRIDGE

NEWTON LA

WENSLEYDALE RD

ARN
DALE

PEAKDALE

Seven Oaks
Farm

1

LITTLE DALE

SNOWDENS

WHITESLATES FIELD

HALLESLADE

BARROW CL

BRONZE

BLACKWELL
CL

COVERDALE
RD

HERRICK WAY

PORTGATE

BUTT

GUTHLAXTON

NEWTON LA

Highfield
Farm

98

HEARDS CL

STANBRIG

SIMONS
CL

IMABLOWE

FIELD

Wigston
Harcourt

Spring
Cottage
Farm

A

62

B

C

HOSKINS CL

Norwood
House

A B Green's Lodge C

Little Acre

Sand & Gravel Pit

98

Cemy

Springfield Farm

L Ctr

4

SPORTS FIELD LA
LODGE CL
COMPTON DR
FOREST RD
CRITCHLOW RD
DENMAN LA
LANGLEY CL
HOBILL CL
BENNETT RISE

CHENEY CT 1
EUNICE AVE 2

Huncote Com Prim Sch

Huncote

1
CHENEY END
CHANTRY CL
MILL VIEW CL
2

DUNCAN DR
Liby
COOPER CL

SCHOOL LA
CRITCHLEY CL
ROBOTHAM CL

Thurlaston Brook

MAIN ST
PO
PH
BROOK ST

THE GREEN

Stone Quarry

Mill

NARBOROUGH RD

ST JAMES CL
CAREY RD
RATCLIFFE DR

Elms Farm

CROFT HILL RD

LE9

3

THURLASTON LA

97

2

Croft Hill

Croft Quarry

HUNCOTE RD

1

MARSTON RD

THE GREEN
HILL ST
DOVECOTE RD

Works

96

Cemy

PH

STATION RD

A

5 TERRACE COTTS

92

B

MARION'S WAY

Fosse Farm

52

C

B4114

SHADES CL
WINSTON
ARBOR RD
CONISTON WAY
BALA
WINDERM
KENDALL
COLLIERS

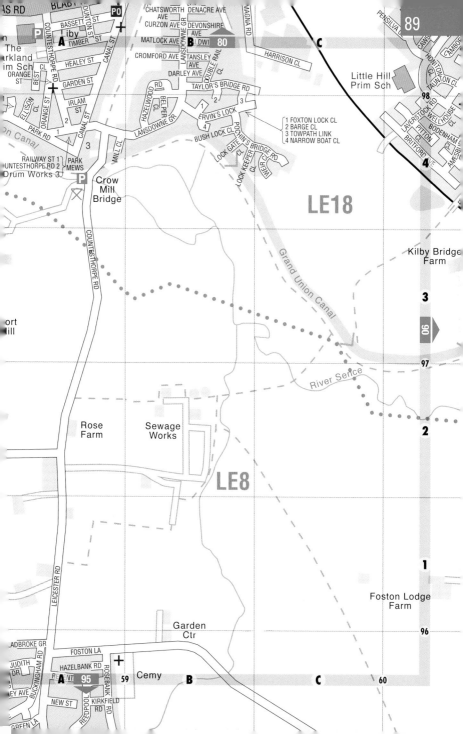

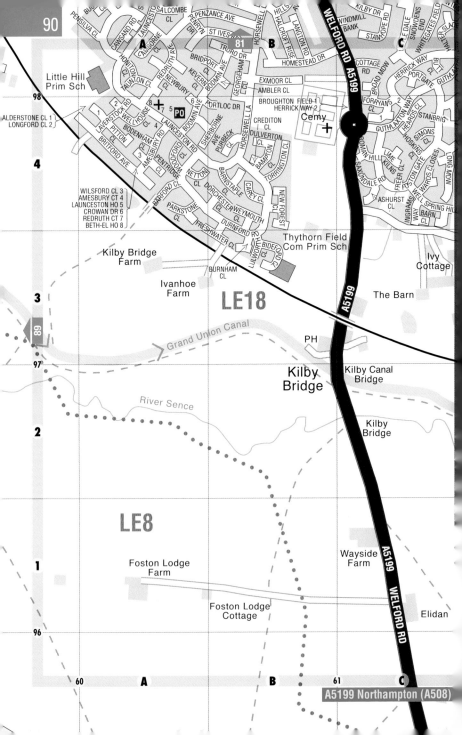

Little Hill Prim Sch

98

ALDERSTONE CL 1
LONGFORD CL 2

4

PENSILVA CL
CAMSAND RD
LAUNCESTO
SALCOMBE CL
PENZANCE AVE
HORSEWELL HILLS
HALCROFT RISE
WELFORD RD A5199
KILBY DR
WINDMILL BANK
STANHOPE RD
E DALE
SNOWDENS END
WHITEGATES FIELD

PENRYN
ST IVES CL
TRURO DR
LANGTON RD
COTTAGE RD
PORTGATE
GUTHA
BRIDPORT CL
KEVERN CL
BODMIN AVE
GEORGEHAM CL
HOMESTEAD DR
BROAD MDW
HERRICK WAY
BUTT

HONITON CL
TAUNTON CL
REDRUTH CL
NEWBURY
EXMOOR CL
AMBLER CL
FORRYAN
CL
ROMAN HILL
GUTHA
STANBRIG

A
CANBORNE CL
PORTLOC DR
BROUGHTON FIELD 1
HERRICK WAY 2
Cemy
SAXONDALE RD
LIME KILNS
SIMONS
CL

1
2
7 8
5 PO
LAVERSTOCK RD
WELLHOUSE
LAUNCESTON RD
SHERBORNE AVE
CREDITON CL
DULVERTON CL
GUTHLAXTON WAY
HEARES CL
HOSKINS
FREER RD
LONG MDW

BODENHAM
PITTON CL
PURBECK
BAMPTON CL
TORRINGTON CL
FOSTON GATE
WARDS CLOSES

BRITFORD AVE
AMESBURY
PENTRIDGE
NETTON
BARNSTAPLE
CAREY CL
ASHURST CL
INGRAMS WAY
WELL SPRING HILL

WILSFORD CL 3
AMESBURY CT 4
LAUNCESTON HO 5
CROWAN DR 6
REDRUTH CT 7
BETH-EL HO 8

BARFORD CL
DORCHESTER
WEYMOUTH CL
NEW FOREST CL
BARN
WAY

PARKSTONE CL
DURNFORD RD
FRESHWATER CL
BIDEFORD

Kilby Bridge Farm

Ivanhoe Farm
BURNHAM CL
LULWORTH CL

Thythorn Field Com Prim Sch

Ivy Cottage

3
68
89
97

LE18

Grand Union Canal

PH

The Barn

2

River Sence

Kilby Bridge

Kilby Canal Bridge

Kilby Bridge

LE8

1

Foston Lodge Farm

Wayside Farm

Foston Lodge Cottage

Elidan

96

60
A
B
61
C

A5199 WELFORD RD

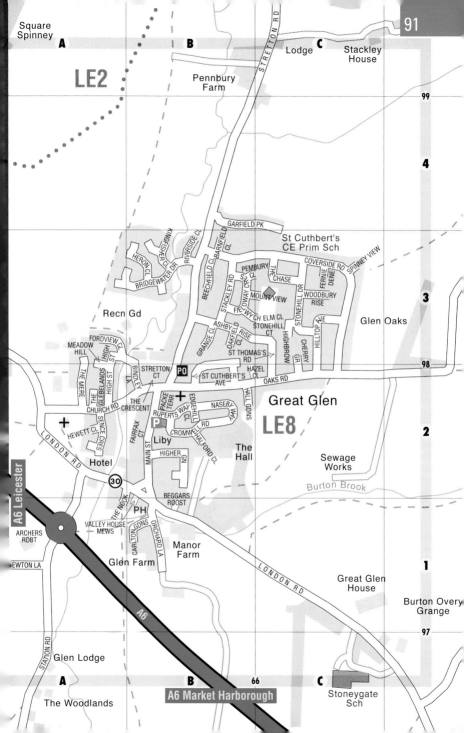

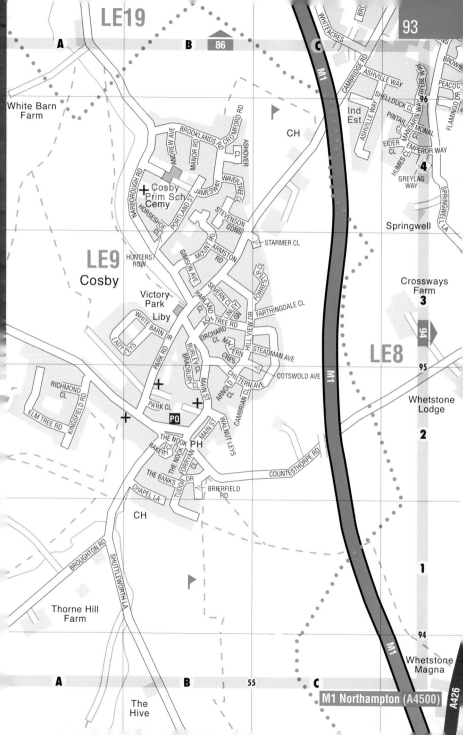

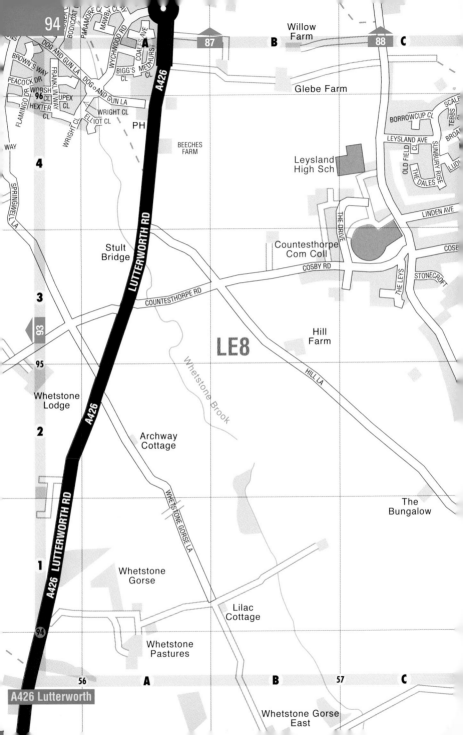

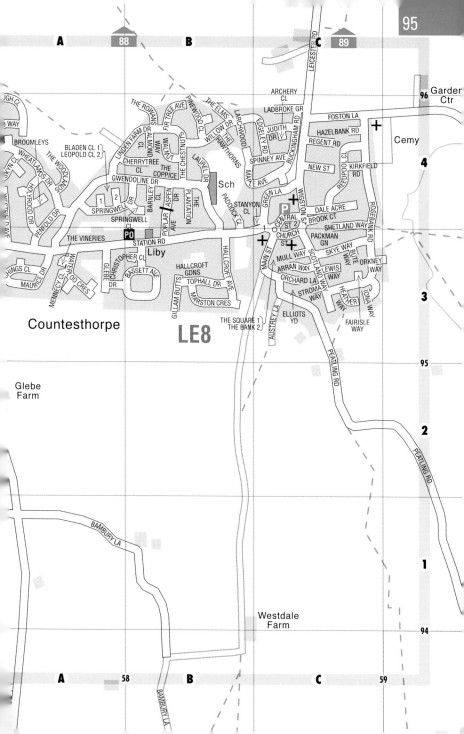

A　　　　　**B**　　　　　**C**

88　　　　　89

Garder Ctr

96

Cemy

4

THE ROWANS
FIR TREE AVE
PINEWOOD CL
THE ELMS
LARCHWOOD
WILLOW DR
THE HAWTHORNS
ALMOND WAY
WALNUT
THE CHESTNUTS
LAUREL DR
EDGELEY RD
JUDITH DR
SPINNEY AVE
MAPLE AVE
BUCKINGHAM RD
ARCHERY CL
LADBROKE GR
FOSTON LA
HAZELBANK RD
REGENT RD
NEW ST
REDPOOL CL
KIRKFIELD RD
ROSEBANK RD

BLADEN CL 1
LEOPOLD CL 2
LINDEN FARM DR
CHERRYTREE CL
THE COPPICE
GWENDOLINE DR
BARNLEY CL
ASPEN DR
POPLAR AVE
THE PLANTATION
PADDOCK CL
STANYON CL
GREEN LA

BROOMLEYS
WHEATLANDS DR
THE WOODLANDS
HOLYROOD DR
PENFOLD DR
SPRINGWELL CL
SPRINGWELL DR
THE VINERIES
STATION RD
Liby

WAY
GH CL
WAY

Sch

1　2
1

P

CENTRAL ST 27
CHURCH
WILSON ST
DALE ACRE
BROOK CT
SHETLAND WAY
PACKMAN GN
SKYE WAY
BUTE WAY
ORKNEY WAY

3

HINGS CL
MAURICE DR
MENNECY CL
WATERLOO CRES
GLEBE DR
CHRISTOPHER CL
BASSETT AVE
HALLCROFT GDNS
TOPHALL DR
HALLCROFT AVE
GILLAM BUTTS
MARSTON CRES

MAIN ST
MULL WAY
ARRAN WAY
SCOTLAND WAY
LEWIS WAY
ORCHARD LA
STROMAY WAY
HEATHER WAY
IONA WAY
FAIRISLE WAY

Countesthorpe

LE8

THE SQUARE 1
THE BANK 2

AUSTREY LA

ELLIOTS YD

PEATLING RD

95

Glebe Farm

2

PEATLING RD

BAMBURY LA

1

Westdale Farm

94

A　　58　　**B**　　　　**C**　　59

BAMBURY LA

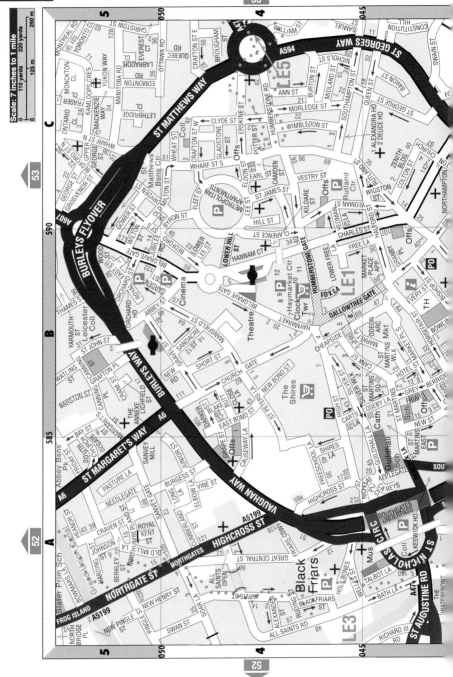

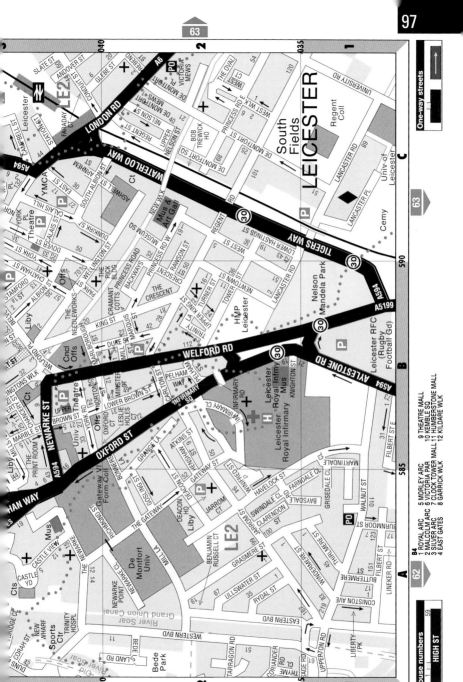

LEICESTER

South Fields

One-way streets

House numbers 59

HIGH ST

B4
1 ROYAL ARC
2 VICTORIA PARADE ARC
3 SILVER ARC
4 EAST GATES
5 MORLEY ARC
6 VICTORIA PAR
7 CLOCK TOWER MALL
8 GARRICK WLK
9 THEATRE MALL
10 KEMBLE SQ
11 HUMBERSTONE MALL
12 KILDARE WLK

Leicester Royal Infirmary

Leicester Royal Infmy Mus

HMP Leicester

Nelson Mandela Park

Leicester RFC (Rugby Football Gd)

De Montfort Univ

Gateway VI Form Coll

Bede Park

River Soar Grand Union Canal

Univ of Leicester

Regent Coll

Mus & Art Gall

Palais Theatre

The Pick Bldg

The Crescent

The Needleworks

Cncl Offs

Univ Theatre

Sports Ctr

Liberty PK

Index

Street names are listed alphabetically and show the locality, the Postcode district, the page number and a reference to the square in which the name falls on the map page

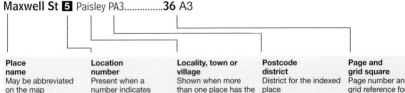

Maxwell St **5** Paisley PA3..............**36** A3

Place name	Location number	Locality, town or village	Postcode district	Page and grid square
May be abbreviated on the map	Present when a number indicates the place's position in a crowded area of mapping	Shown when more than one place has the same name	District for the indexed place	Page number and grid reference for the standard mapping

Towns and villages are listed in CAPITAL LETTERS
Public and commercial buildings are highlighted in magenta. **Places of interest** are highlighted in blue with a star*

Abbreviations used in the index

Acad	**Academy**	Ct	**Court**	Hts	**Heights**	Pl	**Place**
App	**Approach**	Ctr	**Centre**	Ind	**Industrial**	Prec	**Precinct**
Arc	**Arcade**	Ctry	**Country**	Inst	**Institute**	Prom	**Promenade**
Ave	**Avenue**	Cty	**County**	Int	**International**	Rd	**Road**
Bglw	**Bungalow**	Dr	**Drive**	Intc	**Interchange**	Recn	**Recreation**
Bldg	**Building**	Dro	**Drove**	Junc	**Junction**	Ret	**Retail**
Bsns, Bus	**Business**	Ed	**Education**	L	**Leisure**	Sh	**Shopping**
Bvd	**Boulevard**	Emb	**Embankment**	La	**Lane**	Sq	**Square**
Cath	**Cathedral**	Est	**Estate**	Liby	**Library**	St	**Street**
Cir	**Circus**	Ex	**Exhibition**	Mdw	**Meadow**	Sta	**Station**
Cl	**Close**	Gd	**Ground**	Meml	**Memorial**	Terr	**Terrace**
Cnr	**Corner**	Gdn	**Garden**	Mkt	**Market**	TH	**Town Hall**
Coll	**College**	Gn	**Green**	Mus	**Museum**	Univ	**University**
Com	**Community**	Gr	**Grove**	Orch	**Orchard**	Wk, Wlk	**Walk**
Comm	**Common**	H	**Hall**	Pal	**Palace**	Wr	**Water**
Cott	**Cottage**	Ho	**House**	Par	**Parade**	Yd	**Yard**
Cres	**Crescent**	Hospl	**Hospital**	Pas	**Passage**		
Cswy	**Causeway**	HQ	**Headquarters**	Pk	**Park**		

Index of towns, villages, streets, hospitals, industrial estates, railway stations, schools, shopping centres, universities and places of interest

Abb–Alm

A

Abberton Way LE11 .... 6 A2
Abbey Bsns Pk LE4 ...52 C3
Abbey Court Rd LE4..43 B3
Abbey Ct LE4 .... 43 B2
Abbey Dr LE4......... 43 B3
Abbey Gate LE4.......52 C3
Abbey La LE4.......... 43 B2
Abbey Mdws LE4 .....43 B1
Abbeymead Rd LE4 .. 43 B3
ABBEY PARK 53 A4
Abbey Park Rd LE4 ...53 A4
Abbey Park St LE4 ....53 B4
Abbey Prim Com Sch
LE4 ....43 C1
Abbey Rd LE19.........77 B1
Abbey Rise LE4........43 B3
Abbey St LE1 ....96 B5
Abbots Cl LE5 ....55 C4
Abbots Ct LE5 ....55 C4
Abbotsford Cl LE7 ...57 A4
Abbotsford Rd LE5...55 A3
Abbot's Rd N LE5 ....55 C4

Abbots Rd S LE5 ......56 A4
Abbotts Cl LE7........30 B3
Aberdale Rd LE2......71 C2
Aber Rd LE2 ....64 B2
Abingdon Rd LE2 ....63 C4
Abington High Sch
LE18.................81 A2
Abney St LE5 ....64 A4
Acacia Ave LE4 ....35 C4
Acacia Cl LE3.........59 A2
Acan Way LE19 ....85 B3
Acer Cl
Leicester LE4 ....42 B4
Loughborough LE11 ...12 A3
Narborough LE19.......85 B3
Acorn Cl LE4 ....35 B2
Acorn Grange **2** LE11 . 7 C2
Acorn St LE4 ....44 A2
Acorn Way LE18 .....81 C2
Acres Rd LE3 ....59 B3
Adam Dale LE11.......8 A3
Adcock Rd LE3........51 C3
Adcocks Cl LE11......4 B1
Adderley Rd LE2......63 C1
Adelaide Cl LE4.......34 A3
Adkins Ct LE12 ....14 C4
Adlington Rd LE2 ....74 A2
Afton Cl LE11.........6 B3

Agar St LE4...........44 A2
Aikman Ave LE3 ......51 C3
Aikman Cl LE3........51 B3
Aingarth LE11 .... 8 C3
Ainsdale Rd LE3 .....51 C1
Ainsworth Dr LE12 ..19 B4
Ainsworth Wlk LE3 ..51 B1
Aintree Cl LE5........66 B4
Aintree Cres LE2......73 A2
Aisne Rd LE18 ....79 C3
Alan Cl LE4...........44 A4
Alan Moss Rd LE11...3 C1
Albany St LE11 .... 3 B1
Albany The LE7.......64 A3
Alberta St LE5........53 C2
Albert Ave LE12......19 A4
Albert Ct
Leicester LE2 ....64 B2
Whetstone LE8........87 A4
Albert Pl LE11 .... 8 B3
Albert Prom LE11 .... 8 C3
Albert Rd LE2.........64 A2
Albert St
Loughborough LE11 ... 8 B3
Syston LE7 ....31 A3
Albion Ct LE2.........73 B1
Albion Par LE7 ....31 A3
Albion Rd LE12......18 C2

Albion St
Anstey LE7 ....32 C2
Leicester LE1 ....97 B3
Leicester, Oadby LE2 ..73 B1
Syston LE7 ....31 A3
Wigston LE18 ....80 A4
Alcester Dr LE5.......66 B4
Alcott Cl LE3 ....61 B4
Aldeby Cl
Leicester LE2 ....78 C4
Narborough LE19.......77 C2
Alder Cl LE3...........59 A2
Alderleigh Rd LE2 ...79 C1
Alderman Richard
Hallam Prim Sch
LE4 ....42 B1
Alderstone Cl LE18 ..90 A4
Alderton Cl LE4.......36 A1
Aldgate Ave LE5 .....65 C3
Alexander Ave LE19..76 B3
Alexander Rd LE12...13 C3
Alexander St LE3 .....96 A4
Alexandra Bldg LE18.80 C2
Alexandra Ct LE2 ....73 C1
Alexandra Ho LE1....96 C4
Alexandra Rd LE2....64 B1
Alexandra St
Narborough LE19 .....86 A4

Alexandra St *continued*
Thurmaston LE4 ......36 C4
Alfred St LE11 .... 4 B1
Alfreton Rd LE18......81 A4
Alice Gdns LE8 ....87 A1
Allandale Rd LE2 .....64 C1
Allen Ave LE12........13 C3
Allendale Rd LE11 ...12 B3
Allerton Dr LE3........41 C1
Allenwood Rd LE2 ...79 C4
Allexton Gdns LE3 ...50 B2
Alliance Rd LE3.......50 A3
Allington Dr LE4......35 C4
Allington St LE4 ......53 C4
Allinson Cl LE5 ....55 B2
Alloway Cl LE4........44 C4
All Saints CE Prim Sch
LE18.................81 A2
All Saints Open LE1...96 A4
All Saints Rd
Leicester LE3 ....96 A4
Thurcaston LE7.......27 A2
Allsopp's La LE11......5 A1
Alma St LE3 ....52 A3
Almond Cl
Countesthorpe LE8....95 B4
Loughborough LE11 ..12 A2
Almond Rd LE2 ....63 A3

Orsett Cl LE5 55 B4
Orson Dr LE18 80 C3
Orson St LE5 54 B1
Orton Rd LE4 43 B3
Orwell Cl LE11 3 A2
Orwell Dr LE4 41 C4
Osborne Rd
  Leicester LE5 54 B1
  Loughborough LE11 2 C2
Osbourne Ct LE8 87 A4
Osiers Business Pk The LE19 68 C2
Osiers The
  Braunstone Town LE3 69 A3
  Loughborough LE11 12 A3
  Mountsorrel LE12 16 C1
Osmaston Rd LE5 64 B4
Osprey Rd LE4 33 B2
Osterley Cl LE11 6 C4
Oswin Rd LE3 50 C1
Ottawa Rd LE1 96 C4
Otter La LE12 17 C2
Otter Way LE8 87 A1
Our Lady's Convent Sch LE11 8 B2
Outfields Dr LE7 26 B2
Outwood Cl LE3 50 B1
Outwoods Ave LE11 7 C1
Outwoods Dr LE11 7 C1
Outwoods Edge Prim Sch LE11 12 A3
Out Woods Nature Reserve* LE11 10 C1
Outwoods Nature Trail The* LE11 10 C1
Outwoods Rd LE11 11 C4
Oval The
  Leicester LE1 97 C2
  Leicester, Oadby LE2 82 A4
Overdale Ave LE3 40 A3
Overdale Cl LE7 40 A2
Overdale Inf Sch LE2 72 A2
Overdale Jun Sch LE2 72 A3
Overdale Rd
  Leicester LE2 72 A3
  Thurmaston LE4 37 A2
Overfield Cl
  Narborough LE19 85 B3
  Ratby LE6 48 B4
Overfield Wlk LE6 38 C1
Overing Cl LE4 43 C3
Overpark Ave LE3 61 B3
Overseal Rd LE3 50 C4
Overton Rd LE5 54 B3
Owen Cl
  Braunstone Town LE3 60 B1
  Leicester LE4 36 C1
Owston Dr LE18 80 C3
Oxburgh Cl LE11 2 C1
Oxendon St LE2 53 C1
Oxendon Wlk 9 LE2 53 C1
Oxford Ave LE2 63 C3
Oxford Ct
  Leicester LE1 97 B2
  Syston LE7 31 B4
Oxford Dr LE18 80 A2
Oxford Rd LE2 63 C2
Oxford St
  Leicester LE1 97 B2
  Loughborough LE11 7 C4
  Syston LE7 31 B3
Oxon Way LE5 55 B2
Oxted Rise LE2 82 B3

P

Packer Ave LE3 59 C4
Packe St LE11 8 A4
Packe Terr LE8 91 B2
Packhorse Dr LE19 77 B2
Packhorse Gn LE2 79 B3
Pack Horse La LE11 8 B3
Packhorse Rd LE2 79 B3
Packman Gn LE8 95 C3
Packwood Rd LE4 43 A3
Paddock Cl
  Countesthorpe LE8 95 B4
  Leicester, Oadby LE2 73 A2
  Quorn (Quorndon) LE12 14 B1
  Rothley LE7 21 B1
Paddock St LE18 81 B2
Paddocks The LE19 86 B3
Paddock View LE7 30 B3
Padgate Cl LE7 57 A2
Padstow Rd LE4 45 A3
Padwell La LE7 67 B4
Paget Ave LE4 35 C3
Paget Rd LE3 52 B2
Paget St
  Leicester LE2 70 A2
  Loughborough LE11 7 C4
Paigle Rd LE2 70 A2
Painter St LE1 53 B4
Palfreyman La LE2 83 C4
Palmer Ave LE11 3 C1
Palmer St LE4 43 C3
Palmerston Bvd LE2 72 A2
Palmerston Way LE2 72 B2
Palms Pk LE11 3 A1
Pamela Pl LE4 43 A4
Pankhurst Rd LE4 33 C2
Pantain Rd LE11 7 C1
Paper Mill Cl LE7 32 B2
Parade The
  Glen Parva LE2 78 B2
  Leicester, Oadby LE2 73 B2
Paramore Cl LE8 87 B1
Parham Cl LE3 42 A1
Park Ave
  Leicester LE2 70 C4
  Loughborough LE11 8 B1
Park Cl LE9 93 B2
Park Cres LE2 83 A4
Park Ct LE11 8 B2
Parkdale Rd LE4 36 C2
Park Dr
  Braunstone Town LE3 60 A3
  Glenfield LE3 50 A4
Parker Dr LE4 43 A2
Parkers Fields LE12 14 A3
Parkfield Cl LE6 48 B4
Parkhill LE2 70 B4
Park Hill Ave LE2 70 B3
Park Hill Dr LE2 70 B4
Park House Cl LE4 35 B1
Park House Ct LE8 87 C4
Park La LE2 64 B2
Parkland Dr LE2 73 B2
Parkland Prim Sch The LE18 80 A1
Parklands Ave LE6 38 C3
Parklands Dr LE11 12 A4
Park Mews LE18 89 A4
Park Rd
  Anstey LE7 32 B1
  Birstall LE4 35 A2
  Blaby LE8 87 C4
  Cosby LE9 93 B3
  Loughborough LE11 8 B2
  Loughborough, Shelthorpe LE11 12 A4
  Narborough LE19 85 C3
  Ratby LE6 48 B3
  Sileby LE12 18 C4
  Wigston LE18 89 A4
Park Rise LE3 50 C1
Parkside LE6 39 B4
Parkside Cl LE4 33 B2
Parks Prim Sch LE3 51 B4
Park St
  Leicester LE1 97 B3
  Loughborough LE11 8 B3
Parkstone Cl LE18 90 A4
Parkstone Rd
  Leicester LE5 56 B4
  Syston LE7 24 B1
Park The LE2 63 C3
Park Vale Rd LE5 54 A1
Park View LE3 50 C1
Park View Riding Sch* LE7 26 C1
Parkway The LE5 55 C3
Parlour Cl LE18 81 A2
Parnell Cl LE19 86 A2
Parry St LE5 54 A3
Parsons Dr
  Glen Parva LE2 78 B3
  Sileby LE12 19 B4
Partridge Cl
  Mountsorrel LE12 17 C2
  Syston LE7 30 B4
Partridge Rd LE4 37 A2
Parvian Rd LE2 80 B4
Pasley Cl LE2 79 B4
Pasley Rd LE2 79 B4
Pasture La LE1 96 A5
Pastures Prim Sch The LE19 76 A2
Pastures The
  Barrow-u-S LE12 15 B2
  Leicester, Oadby LE2 83 C4
  Narborough LE19 76 B1
  Syston LE7 30 A3
Paterson Cl LE4 33 C2
Paton St LE3 62 B4
Patterdale Dr LE11 6 C1
Patterdale Rd LE4 36 C2
Paul Dr LE4 45 B4
Pauline Ave LE4 44 A4
Pavilion Way LE11 4 A2
Pawley Cl LE8 87 B2
Pawley Gdns LE2 79 B4
Pawley Gn LE2 79 B4
Payne St LE4 44 A3
Peacock Dr LE8 87 A1
Peacock La LE1 96 A3
Peakdale LE18 82 A1
Peake Rd LE4 44 C1
Peartree Cl
  Anstey LE7 32 B1
  Glenfield LE3 49 C3
Pear Tree La LE11 2 A2
Pear Tree Way LE11 2 B2
Peashill Cl LE12 19 B3
Peatling Rd LE8 95 C2
Pedlars Cl LE4 42 A3
Peebles Way LE4 44 C3
Peel Dr LE11 8 C4
Peewit Cl LE2 78 B3
Pegasus Cl LE2 53 C1
Peggs La LE7 25 C1
Peldon Cl LE4 42 C2
Pelham St
  Leicester LE1 97 B2
  Leicester, Oadby LE2 73 B2
Pelham Way LE1 97 B2
Pell Cl LE12 15 B4
Pembroke Ave
  Syston LE7 31 B2
  Wigston LE18 80 A2
Pembroke St LE5 54 A3
Pembury Cl LE8 91 B3
Pen Cl LE2 79 C4
Pendene Rd LE2 64 A1
Pendlebury Dr LE2 71 B3
Pendragon Way LE3 59 B2
Penfold Dr LE8 95 A4
Penhale Rd LE3 69 A4
Penkridge Wlk LE4 43 A4
Penman Way LE19 68 C1
Pennant Cl LE3 50 B3
Penney Cl LE18 81 A3
Pennine Cl LE2 74 B1
Penny Long La LE3 59 A3
Penrith Rd LE4 44 B2
Penryn Dr LE18 81 A1
Pensilva Cl LE18 81 A1
Pentridge Cl LE18 90 A4
Penzance Ave LE18 81 B1
Peppercorn Cl LE4 42 C3
Pepper Dr LE12 13 C3
Pepper's Cl LE12 17 A4
Percival St LE5 54 B3
Percy Rd LE2 70 C3
Percy St LE3 69 B4
Peregrine Rise LE4 33 B2
Perkyn Rd LE5 56 B2
Perry Gr LE11 8 C1
Perseverance Rd LE4 35 B1
Perth Ave LE3 51 B3
Peters Dr LE5 55 C3
Petersfield LE9 92 B4
Petunia Cl LE3 59 A2
Petworth Dr
  Leicester LE3 51 C2
  Loughborough LE11 2 C1
Pevensey Ave LE5 66 B3
Pevensey Rd LE11 3 B1
Peverel Ct LE3 60 C1
Peverel Rd LE3 61 B2
Phillip Dr LE2 79 C1
Phillips Cres LE4 33 C2
Phipps Cl LE8 87 B2
Phoenix Cl LE3 51 C3
Phoenix Dr LE12 19 A2
Piccaver Rise LE3 50 B2
Pick Bldg The LE1 97 B3
Pickering Cl LE4 44 C1
Pickhill Rd LE5 46 C3
Pickwell Cl LE3 50 C4
Piers Rd LE3 40 B1
Pilgrim Gdns LE5 65 B3
Pilkington Rd LE3 60 C3
Pimpernel Cl LE19 76 A1
Pindar Rd LE3 51 B3
Pine Cl LE11 12 A3
Pine Dr LE7 31 A2
Pinehurst Cl LE3 50 A2
Pine Rd LE3 50 A4
Pines The LE7 67 C4
Pine Tree Ave
  Groby LE6 39 B2
  Leicester LE5 55 B4
Pine Tree Cl LE2 82 C4
Pine Tree Gdn LE2 82 C4
Pine Tree Gr LE9 58 C2
Pine View LE3 59 C4
Pinewood Ave LE4 36 C2
Pinewood Cl
  Countesthorpe LE8 95 B4
  Leicester LE4 33 B1
Pinfold LE3 69 A3
Pinfold Gate LE11 8 B4
Pinfold Gdns LE11 8 B4
Pinfold Jetty 6 LE11 8 B4
Pinfold Rd LE4 36 B2
Pinfold The LE6 48 A4
Pingle St LE3 96 A5
Pingle The LE12 13 B1
Piper Cl
  Leicester LE3 51 B3
  Loughborough LE11 7 C1
Piper Way LE3 51 B3
Pipewell Wlk 2 LE4 43 A3
Pipistrelle Way LE2 83 C4
Pitchens Cl LE4 33 A1
Pits Ave LE3 68 C3
Pitsford Dr LE11 6 A2
Pitton Cl LE18 90 A4
Plain Gate LE7 20 C4
Plantation Ave LE2 70 A2
Plantation The LE8 95 B4
Platts La LE7 22 C3
Player Cl LE4 36 B1
Pleasant Cl
  Leicester Forest East LE3 59 A2
  Loughborough LE11 8 A4
Plough Cl
  Leicester Forest East LE3 59 A1
  Mountsorrel LE12 21 A4
Ploughman's Lea LE7 25 A3
Plover Cres LE4 33 C2
Plowman Cl LE3 40 B1
Plumtree Cl LE11 3 C2
Plumtree Way LE7 31 A3
Pluto Cl LE2 53 C1
Plymouth Dr LE5 65 A4
Plymstock Cl LE3 51 C2
Poachers Cl LE3 49 C4
Poachers Pl LE2 83 B4
Pochin's Bridge Rd LE18 89 B4
Pochins Cl LE18 81 A1
Pochin St LE9 92 A4
Pochin Way LE12 19 A4
Pocket End LE11 11 B4
Pocklingtons Wlk LE1 97 B3
Polaris Cl LE2 53 C1
Polebrook Cl LE3 41 A3
Pollard Ct LE2 64 B2
Pollard Rd LE3 60 C3
Pomeroy Dr LE2 73 A1
Pool Rd LE3 52 A2
Pope Cres LE19 76 B3
Pope St LE2 71 B4
Poplar Ave
  Birstall LE4 35 B3
  Countesthorpe LE8 95 B4
Poplar Rd
  Littlethorpe LE19 85 C2
  Loughborough LE11 12 B3
Poplars Cl LE6 39 A3
Poplars The
  Leicester LE3 69 B3
  Ratby LE6 38 A1
Poppins The LE4 33 C2
Poppy Cl
  Groby LE6 39 C3
  Leicester LE2 80 A4
  Loughborough LE11 12 A2
Porlock St LE3 51 C1
Portcullis Rd LE5 47 A1
Portgate LE18 81 C1
Portishead Rd LE5 54 C4
Portland Rd
  Kirby Fields LE9 58 C4
  Leicester LE2 64 A1
Portland St LE9 93 B4
Portland Twrs LE2 72 C4
Portland Wlk LE2 83 A3
Portloc Dr LE18 90 B4
Portman St LE4 44 A2
Portmore Cl LE4 42 B2
Portsdown Rd LE2 72 B2
Portslade Ho LE3 50 A2
Portsmouth Rd LE4 44 A1
Portwey The LE5 55 A4
Post Rd LE4 30 A1
Pott Acre LE7 17 C1
Potter St LE1 96 C4
Potterton Rd LE4 42 C3
Poulteney Dr LE12 13 C2
Powys Ave LE2 64 C1
Powys Gdns LE2 64 C1
Poynings Ave LE3 51 B2
Prebend St LE2 63 C4
Premier Drum Works LE18 89 A4
Prestbury Rd LE11 6 B4
Preston Cl
  Ratby LE6 48 C4
  Sileby LE12 18 C2
Preston Rise LE5 46 B1
Prestwold Rd LE5 54 B4
Pretoria Cl LE4 34 A3
Pretoria Rd LE9 48 B1
Prevost Gdns LE12 14 A2
Price Way LE4 37 B3
Priestley Rd LE3 61 B4
Priestman Rd LE3 60 A1
Primrose Cl
  Groby LE6 39 C3
  Narborough LE19 85 B4
Primrose Hill LE2 73 A2
Primrose Way
  Kirby Muxloe LE9 49 A2
  Queniborough LE7 25 B2
Prince Albert Dr LE3 50 A3
Prince Dr LE2 74 A1
Princes Cl LE7 32 C2
Princess Ave LE2 83 A4
Princess Ct LE11 4 A2
Princess Dr LE9 58 B4
Princess Rd E LE1 97 C2
Princess Rd W LE1 97 C2
Princess Road Backways LE1 97 B2
Princess St
  Loughborough LE11 8 B3
  Narborough LE19 86 A4
Prince William Rd LE11 4 A2
Prince William Way LE11 4 A2
Print Room The LE1 97 B3
Priory Cl LE7 30 B3
Priory Cres LE3 50 C1
Priory Rd LE11 11 B4
Priory Wlk LE3 59 B3
Proctor's Park Rd LE12 14 C3
Progress Way LE4 45 C3
Prospect Hill LE5 54 A2
Prospect Rd LE5 54 B2
Pryor Rd LE12 19 A4
Pulford Dr LE7 57 B2
Pullman Rd LE18 80 C2

List of numbered locations

In some busy areas of the maps it is not always possible to show the name of every place.

Where not all names will fit, some smaller places are shown by a number. If you wish to find out the name associated with a number, use this listing.

The places in this list are also listed normally in the Index.

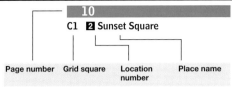

10

C1 **2** Sunset Square

Page number | Grid square | Location number | Place name

7
C2 **1** Berts Coote Ho
2 Acorn Grange
3 Cherry Croft

8
A4 **1** Greenclose La
2 Orchard St
3 Brook Side
4 Ashby Sq
5 Derby Sq
6 Tanni Gray Ho
B4 **1** Warner's La
2 Dead La
3 Churchgate Mews
4 Needleworks The
5 City Hts
6 Pinfold Jetty
C3 **1** Limetree Gr
2 Queen St

18
C3 **1** Old Tannery Dr
2 Simons Wlk
3 Lawson Cl
4 Willet Cl
5 Cygnet Cl
6 Jordean Ct

43
A3 **1** Greystoke Wlk
2 Pipewell Wlk
3 Kirkstead Wlk
4 Chilcombe Wlk
5 Bretton Wlk
6 Canonsleigh Wlk
7 Shelford Wlk
8 Robertsbridge Wlk
B3 **1** Millbrook Wlk
2 Waingroves Wlk
3 Langley Wlk
4 Grovebury Wlk
5 Melcombe Wlk
6 Kirkscroft Wlk

44
A1 **1** Canterbury Ho

46
B3 **1** Lakeview Ct
2 Craneley Ct
3 Belgrave Ct
4 Granby Ct
5 Blacksmith Pl

52
B1 **1** Frederick Jackson Ho

2 Arundel St
3 Andrewes Wlk
4 Norfolk Ho
5 Musgrove Cl
6 Coventry St
7 Earl Howe Terr

53
B3 **1** Foundry La
2 Memory La
3 Foundry Sq
4 Shackleton St
5 St Marks St
6 Melton St
7 Junction Rd
8 Russell Sq
C1 **1** Gordon Ho
2 Clipstone Ho
3 Maxfield Ho
4 Hydra Wlk
5 Framland Ho
6 Len Hollis Ct
7 Goscote Ho
8 Mercury Cl
9 Oxendon Wlk
10 Willow Ct
11 Guthlaxton Ave
12 Maidstone Ho
13 Azad Ho

62
B4 **1** West St Open
2 River Bldg The
3 River Soar Living

63
B1 **1** Strand The
2 Fleetwood Ct
C4 **1** Brookhouse St
2 Brookhouse Ave
3 Andrew Ct
4 Tichborne Ct
5 Salisbury Ave
6 Mandora La
7 Woodbine Ave
8 Gordon Ave
9 St Albans Rd
10 Salisbury Ct
11 Arbor Ct

64
A4 **1** Sutherland St
2 Guilford St
3 Onslow St
4 Conifer Cl
B2 **1** Stoneleigh Manor
2 Stoneycroft

69
A2 **1** Watergate Ct
2 Bannister Rd
A3 **1** Willow Ct
2 Brent Ct
3 Swithland Ct
4 Riseholme Cl
5 Cairns Cl

81
B3 **1** Arcade The
2 Maromme Sq
3 Spring La

96
B4 **1** Royal Arc
2 Malcolm Arc
3 Silver Arc
4 East Gates
5 Morley Arc
6 Victoria Par
7 Clock Tower Mall
8 Garrick Wlk
9 Theatre Mall
10 Kemble Sq
11 Humberstone Mall
12 Kildare Wlk

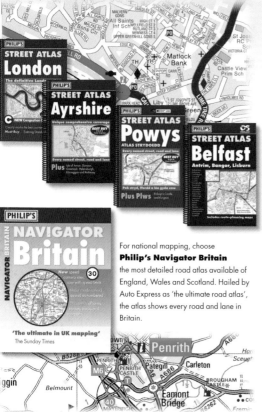